Travel and Tourism

Second Edition

Tutor's Pack

Travel and Tourism

Patrick Lavery

Exercises, cases, notes and other materials to help tutors
extend and support their students' learning.

Second Edition   £39.00 (free with 15+ books bought direct)

Travel and Tourism

Patrick Lavery

Second Edition

Elm Publications

Published April 1990 by ELM Publications,
who hold the copyright on behalf of the author
Dr Patrick Lavery. The first edition was published
in June 1987.

Printed and bound by the St Edmundsbury Press, Suffolk.

British Library Cataloguing in Publication Data

Lavery, Patrick 1942-
    Travel and tourism, - 2nd. ed - (Travel and tourism series,
    ISSN 0952-0296; vol. 2)
    I. Title II. Series
    338.4'791

    ISBN 1-85450-120-8

Contents

List of Tables
List of Figures and Maps
Introduction
About the author

List of Tables

List of Figures & Maps

Introduction

This new and enlarged second edition provides an update on developments in the field of travel and tourism in the later 1980's, and considers issues that will be of importance during the 1990's. For example, topics such as the impact of the Channel tunnel, developments in aircraft technology and future developments in international air travel are considered in greater detail. Chapter 8 has been completely revised and includes an account of the results of the 1989 review of the role and functions of the English Tourist Board. Chapter 13 has been revised and extended to cover timeshare, theme parks, indoor resorts and the impact of new technology in much greater detail.

Patrick Lavery

About the Author

Dr Patrick Lavery is Deputy Director of Humberside College of Higher Education in Hull. He was formerly Head of Tourism at the Dorset Institute of Higher Education. He has taught at the Universities of Liverpool and London and for several years was responsible for tourism planning with the Metropolitan County Council. He has published extensively over the past 20 years and has written many articles on several aspects of tourism research and development. He has also acted as a Consultant on Education and Training for Tourism and has worked for the European Economic Community and the English Tourist Board. He has also presented papers on tourism management at Conferences in Britain, Europe and the United States.

Acknowledgements

My particular thanks go to Mrs A Gifford and Mrs L Drew for their patience and care in typing the finished manuscript, and to Miss P Griffin for some of the line drawings. I would also like to record the help given to me by Derek Robbins who read and commented on Chapter 6, Paul McKeough for his advice and comments on Chapter 9 and Professor Carlton Van Doren for his assistance on updating USA travel statistics. I would also like to thank Sheila Ritchie, my publisher, for commissioning the book and her encouragement to see it through to completion. Finally, I must give special thanks to my wife Alma, for her encouragement and patience over the past twelve months. Without their combined assistance and support, this book would have remained an idea and not a reality.

Chapter 1

The Tourism Industry

Learning Objectives: After reading this chapter and some of the references and tackling one of the assignments you should have a clear idea of:

(i) the nature of the tourist industry
(ii) some data sources about trends in domestic and international tourism.

Introduction: What is Tourism?

Although tourism has existed in a limited form since the Middle Ages, the first definition of the term 'tourist' was made almost 50 years ago by the Council of the League of Nations, (L.N., 1937) and subsequently ratified in 1963 by the United Nations (IUOTO, 1963). The term 'tourist' was taken to mean any person travelling for a period of twenty-four hours or more in a country other than that in which he or she usually resides, for the purpose of leisure, business, family, friends, meeting mission. To this was added the term 'excursionist' to cover people staying less than twenty-four hours in the country visited (Lickorish, 1958).

However, neither definition covers domestic tourism and for this reason the phenomenon should be best described using a Tourism Society definition:

> 'Tourism is the temporary short-term movement of people to destinations outside the places where they normally live and work, and their activities during the stay at these destinations; it includes movement for all purposes as well as day visits or excursions' (D.Airey, 1981).

Tourism then is a unique phenomenon. Unlike other products the tourism product has to be consumed on the spot and the industry is designed to move the market to the product; and in this regard is quite unlike any other form of economic activity. However, tourism is not just an economic phenomenon. It can have social, political and environmental consequences. So tourism is not a simple phenomenon and the types of 'tourist' and the reasons for them being tourists are not always readily apparent. Tourism is rather like the elephant. It is easier to recognise than to define.

What then are the characteristics of tourism? It involves travelling to a destination away from home for the purposes of leisure and pleasure. Tourists may stay in their holiday destination for days or weeks or hours — but in general their activities on arrival are similar — for example sight-seeing, relaxing on a beach, sport, shopping, enjoying the local cuisine or similar pursuits. Often it involves buying a 'package' and this may cover everything from the return journey home to the resort as well as accommodation and meals and organised activities during the stay there.

The industry has developed to meet all the needs of the tourist, and in sequence these are:

(i) Developing tourist destinations/attractions;

(ii)   Promoting and selling these;

(iii) Transporting tourists from their home area/country to the tourist resort;

(iv) Providing them with accommodation during their stay;

(v)   Developing additional leisure activities and tours during their stay;

(vi) Making goods and selling souvenirs of their visits, local crafts, and produce;

(vii) Transporting them home again.

The Tourist Industry

The tourist industry then can be divided into four main sectors each of which has some responsibility for part or all of these activities. These sectors are:-

(i)   **Travel:** including travel agents, tour operators, airlines, cruise companies, coach companies, railways, taxis, tourist guides, couriers, reservations and sales staff.

(ii)   **Accommodation, catering and related services:** Hotels with all their staff from receptionist to chambermaids, chefs and cooks, waiters/waitresses, bar staff, porters, caravan site/camping site staff, self catering enterprises, restaurants and cafes.

(iii) **Leisure facilities and entertainment:** These will include theatres, museums, art galleries, theme parks, zoos, wildlife parks, sports centres, gardens, historic houses, country parks, cinemas.

(iv) **Tourism organisations:** whose aim is to market and monitor the quality and development of the tourist region. These will range from national and regional tourist organisations to staff at local tourist information centres.

It is already clear that the industry is a complex one and it includes many different kinds of occupation — all designed to meet the particular needs of the tourist. As well as being complex, tourism is a major industry. For example, in 1987 it was estimated that in Britain some 1.4 million people worked in jobs directly or indirectly connected with tourism. There are also many temporary and seasonal jobs connected with the industry. The following facts give some guide to the scale of the industry:

- A major retail travel agency has 3,800 staff.
- The 1,800 passengers on QE2 are looked after by a crew of more than 1,200.
- An airline buying a new plane will probably be spending about £7 million.
- The Director of leisure and recreation in the London Borough of Hammersmith and Fulham has a budget of £9 million and 600 staff.
- The National Bus Company was the largest bus company in the world. It had more than 14,500 buses and coaches and employed 52,000 staff.
- 6.5 million Britons bought package holidays overseas from tour operators in 1983 and twice as many foreign visitors came to Britain.
- About 3.1 million Americans visited Britain in 1985.
- In 1983 Brighton earned £29 million from conferences.

Although the industry employs large numbers of people, it mainly consists of small firms, for example, family-run hotels, guest houses or restaurants, small travel agents on the high street, craft shops, taxi services, often supplemented by seasonal staff. At the other end of the scale there are a limited number of very large companies with many thousands on their payrolls.

To sum up, the industry is a complex one and it contains many small firms; it covers both the public and private sector and is very much the mixed economy in action. It is one of the world's major industries. In Britain the United Kingdom earnings from tourism through spending by overseas visitors rose from £95 million in 1954 to £190 million in 1964, rose again steadily to £900 million in 1974 and to over £6 billion in 1987 (ETB, 1988). During this same post-war period the annual number of overseas visitors to the UK has grown from 902,000 to 15.6 million, a growth of 150%. There have been fluctuations in earnings and visitor numbers during this period, as Figures 1 and 2 on pages 4 and 5 illustrate, but the overall long-term trend has been one of growth. Although on this evidence alone tourism has been one of the UK's success stories, it has never been fully recognised.

Domestic Tourism

Although we tend to think of tourism in terms of holidays and travel abroad, there is a major and growing domestic industry catering for both overseas visitors to the UK and British nationals on holiday as well as day visitors to tourist areas. Domestic tourism has also grown significantly over the 10 years, from 114 million visits in 1974 to 140 million in 1984 (BTA, 1985), though again with some peaks and troughs. Earnings from domestic tourism grew from £1.8 billion in 1974 to over £7.7 billion in 1988 (ETB, 1989).

For British holidaymakers staying in the UK the seaside has remained the big attraction over the past 30 years and about two-thirds of these holidays are taken at the seaside (BTA). However, the nature, timing and duration of these holidays has changed, as Chapter 2 outlines.

For overseas visitors the domestic UK holiday is often part of a larger 'package' tour covering several destinations, and the domestic industry is catering for a largely affluent clientele who are attracted to a limited number of tourist destinations and are in Britain for sight-seeing and visiting cultural centres. Such visitors would concentrate on an itinerary that covered London — Oxford — Stratford — Chester — the Lake District and/or Scotland with perhaps York and Cambridge on their return leg to London. The English Tourist Board and the 10 regional boards, as well as the many local resort authorities, all help promote domestic tourism. In this context it is typically the mixed economy in action. The 'industry', which is largely made up of firms in the private sector, relies for much of its promotion and marketing activity on these public sector organisations. This issue is covered at greater length in Chapters 8 and 10.

In 1988 overseas visitors spent £6.3 billion in the United Kingdom at current prices. As Table 1 on page 6 shows, the USA provides the greatest number of overseas visitors from a single country, followed by France and Germany (Trade & Industry, 1989). In 1987 the UK domestic tourist market received over 15.7 million visitors who spent between them over £6,000 million (ETB 1989). The pattern of visits was much the same as in recent years, with holidays accounting for 47 per cent of all visits, business for 21 per cent and visits to friends and relatives 20 per cent. Of those overseas residents visiting the UK for a holiday, 29

Figure 1 : Real Spending by Overseas Visitors to the UK 1979-1988

This chart shows total spending by overseas visitors to the UK (excluding fare payments to British carriers) expressed in constant 1984 prices. Constant prices are obtained by adjusting current tourist spending to take account of annual inflation in the general index of retail prices (all items).

SPENDING
(Millions of £ in 1984 prices)

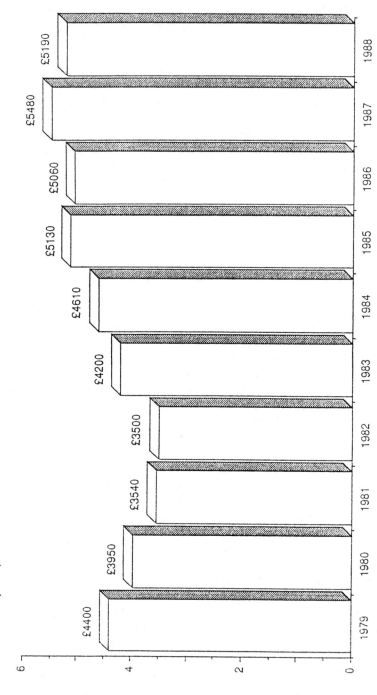

Year	Spending
1979	£4400
1980	£3950
1981	£3540
1982	£3500
1983	£4200
1984	£4610
1985	£5130
1986	£5060
1987	£5480
1988	£5190

Calculations from Business Monitor Series: Overseas Travel and Tourism

Source: International Passenger Survey; adults and children resident abroad.

Figure 2: Numbers of Visitors to the UK from Overseas 1979-1988

This chart shows the number of visits to the UK, in millions, in total and for each main purpose.

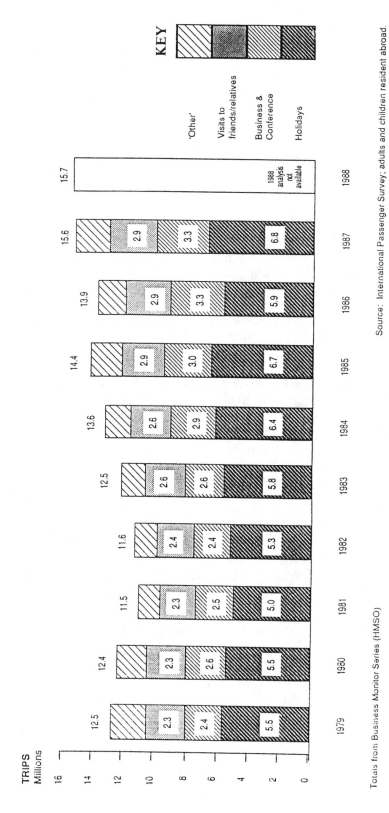

KEY

'Other'

Visits to friends/relatives

Business & Conference

Holidays

Totals from Business Monitor Series (HMSO)

Source: International Passenger Survey; adults and children resident abroad.

per cent came on an inclusive tour and a substantial proportion of those are inclusive tours from North America (BTA, annual). The domestic tourist industry received a boost in 1969 with the *Development of Tourism Act* which set up the British Tourist Authority and Tourist Boards for England, Scotland and Wales with the responsibility for promoting the development of tourism to and within Great Britain (Development of Tourism Act, 1969). The consequences of this Act and the role of these Boards are discussed at length in Chapters 3 and 9, but its significance here is that for the first time the government of the day recognised the importance of the domestic tourist industry.

International Tourism

This refers to travel across National boundaries and may involve visits to one or several other countries. If we analyse the pattern of tourist flows on a world scale it is clear that the industry is a major economic activity. International traveller arrivals amount to 336 million and world spending for international travel amounts to over £75 billion (Waters, 1986). In the developing countries international tourism accounts for about one-third of their service trade. It is one of the fastest-growing industries in the world, and between 1974 and 1980 international tourism trade grew faster than world trade generally. Between 1961 and 1981 the world total of international tourist arrivals quadrupled. However, although the rate of growth of the international tourist has been dramatic, the potential for growth is still substantial. The reason for this is that most of this activity is confined to Europe which accounts for 70 per cent of international tourist arrivals and North America which attracts 20 per cent (WTO, 1986). The rest of the world accounts for only 10 per cent of international tourist arrivals. Table 4 on page 36 and Figures 9 and 10 on pages 38 and 41 show the recent trends in international tourism.

The development of international tourism has produced two types of country — the generating country who provide the tourist and the receiving country who attract and play host to the tourist. A few countries, like Britain, fall into both categories, but most are clearly one type or the other. Generally, the tourist generating countries are those with advanced economies, high standards of living, available disposable income, greater spending power and a general system of paid annual holidays. The most important tourist generating countries are the United States, West Germany, Japan and the United Kingdom.

Table 1
Origin of overseas visitors to UK — 000s

YEAR	AREA OF RESIDENCE			TOTAL ALL VISITS
	North America	Europe	Other Area	
1982	2,135	7,082	2,418	11,636
1983	2,836	7,164	2,464	12,464
1984	3,330	7,551	2,763	13,644
1985	3,797	7,904	2,782	14,493
1987	3,387	9,196	2,855	16,445

Source: *International Passenger Survey*

6

Table 2

Cost of High Season Return

London — New York & Selected Destinations — (£)

Destination (From London — return)	1950	1955	1961	1968
New York	225	187	169	125
Miami	253	215	169	176
Bermuda	252	218	114	118
Mexico	317	250	209	218
San Francisco	326	257	221	246

(Source: Peters, *International Tourism)*

The host countries have a low cost of living, attractive scenery and climates, are readily accessible and have a good public image. As the host countries, such as Spain, Italy and Greece have developed their tourist industry over the past 20 years, so the beaches and main resort areas are reaching saturation point and more developing countries are turning to tourism as a major source of income. Recent years have seen the development of new tourist areas outside of Europe with lower price levels and less tourist saturation.

Given that international tourism is the largest single item in foreign trade, the balance of trade between tourism generating and receiving countries can be a significant element in encouraging economic development. Table 4 shows international tourist receipts and expenditures based on figures supplied by the Organisation for Economic Cooperation and Development (OECD). In Europe, Austria, France, Greece, Italy and Spain, all have net surpluses in their balance of payments, whilst West Germany, the Netherlands, Belgium and the Scandinavian countries have the most marked deficits. Outside of Europe, Japan has the most substantial net deficit and North America has a marked imbalance in its tourist trade.

Trade is a key word in that all countries can use the income from international tourism to create jobs and to buy additional goods and services. In Britain the tourist industry, unlike some other industries, has stood up well to the world recession and has not only maintained but improved its position as a major earner of foreign currency for the UK. In 1987 Britain received 15.3 million overseas visitors and foreign currency earnings, including fares paid to British carriers on travel to and from Britain, amounted to over £6,000 million (ETB, 1988). One example of how trade follows tourism can be seen by foreign visitor spending in British shops. These 12 million visitors are potentially additional customers for British shops and visitor spending on footwear and textiles amounts to £600 million each year, which is equal to almost half of all British footwear and textile exports (DOE, 1986). In the year to December 1987, job numbers in the UK tourist industry increased by 41,000 (ETB, 1988).

Data Sources on Tourism

Clearly, the movement of people between countries and within countries generates a demand for tourism which consists of a range of goods and services provided by

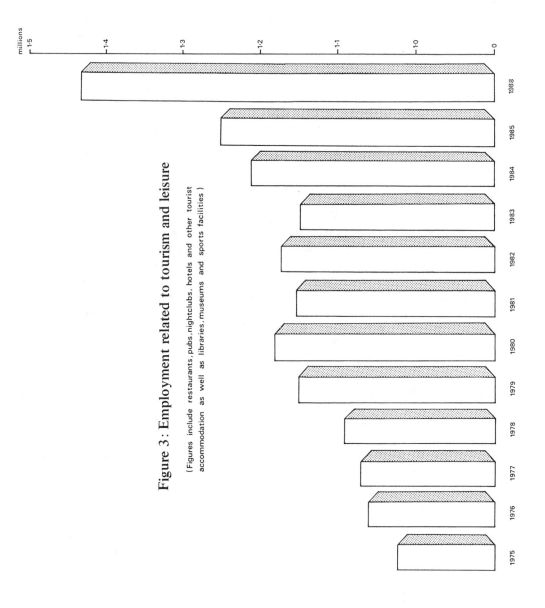

Figure 3 : Employment related to tourism and leisure

(Figures include restaurants, pubs, nightclubs, hotels and other tourist
accommodation as well as libraries, museums and sports facilities)

both the public and private sectors. The income from the sale or purchase of these goods and services may be a major source of foreign or domestic revenue. When many industries or economic activities are examined, detailed statistical data are available on the production, export and import of hundreds of physical goods, often on a monthly basis, yet data on tourism are scarce, often unreliable and not consistently compiled. Part of the reason for this is the substantial time lag which exists between the initial expansion of a sector and the collection of adequate data for that sector. For example, it was not until well into this century that detailed statistics on manufacturing industries became available in many developed countries, although the industrial revolution had transformed the manufacturing sector during the 19th century.

In 1982 White and Walker highlighted the dearth of reliable statistics on tourism, even on an aggregate basis, in some of the more advanced economies (White, 1982). They claimed that some countries may not even be able to tell whether they have a surplus or deficit on their tourism income. Yet, given the importance of tourism as a source of income and employment, it is clear that both the public and private sector need to have detailed statistics on many aspects of tourism. For example, national governments need data on tourist arrivals, countries of origin, visitor spending, mode of travel, purpose of visit, length of stay and places visited. All of this data, analysed over time, is used to provide forecasts in the growth, stability or decline of the tourist industry. Similarly, private firms need such data to plan their marketing strategies and to measure the effectiveness of their existing policies. With this knowledge the public sector will improve road/rail links, plan airport and port expansion schemes and the private sector may develop more hotels or new resort complexes.

International Tourism Surveys: The main sources of data on international tourist flows and the characteristics of international tourism are the annual reports of the Organisation for Economic Cooperation and Development (OECD), and the World Tourism Organisation (WTO).

The OECD was set up in 1960 and its members consist of the countries of Western Europe, Scandinavia, North America, Australia and Japan. The importance of OECD data is that it provides a reliable, standardised and comparable set of statistics for a range of countries who between them account for over 90 per cent of all international tourism. Each year the OECD publishes an annual report containing five main sections:
— recent trends in government policy towards tourism;
— international tourist flows by member country including length of stay, accommodation used and main tourism generating countries;
— the economic importance of international tourism in member countries;
— main types of transport used;
— changes in the accommodation sector.

The WTO publish annually the *World Tourism Statistics Annual Yearbook* (WTO Yearbook), which has a wide range of data on trends in international tourism. It includes data on country of origin, arrivals by month, accommodation, transport, purpose of visit, tourism receipts and hotel accommodation capacity.

In addition to these reports, the *Travel Industry World Yearbook* (Waters, 1988) attempts to provide an overview of trends in world tourism, albeit with a marked North American perspective. It provides a commentary on a very disparate range of tourism data covering all the main centres of tourism activity. Although many of the data sources cited in this yearbook are not directly comparable, it does provide a useful and wide-ranging commentary on trends in international tourism.

The Economist Intelligence Unit publishes four invaluable sources of tourism data. Each quarter the EIU publishes *Country Reports* which provide a business-oriented analysis of the latest political and economic developments in 165 countries worldwide, together with a review of their short term prospects. This data is collated in an annual report which provides a *Country Profile*. On a monthly basis the EIU also publishes a *Business Update* for the ten largest OECD countries. A separate page is devoted to each country and data is provided as industrial trends, financial indicators, consumer demand and related economic indicators. Every three months the EIU publishes the *World Trade Forecast* which provides an integrated view of the world's economic prospects. Finally, the Economist Intelligence Unit publishes the *Travel and Tourism Analyst* on a monthly basis. This contains several in-depth analyses of the main sectors of the travel and tourism industry and topics can range from timeshare to forecasts for long haul travel from Europe to the Caribbean.

National Tourism Surveys: In Britain since 1964 the main source of tourist data has been the International Passenger Survey (IPS). This annual survey is carried out for the Department of Trade and Industry by the Office of Population Censuses and Surveys, and is based on interviews with a stratified random sample of passengers entering and leaving the UK on the principal air and sea routes (IPS annual). Travellers passing through passport control are randomly selected for interview and a sample of over 150,000 interviews provides data on visits and spending by country, purpose of visit, mode of travel, length of stay and places visited in the UK. The results of these surveys are published by the government quarterly and annually in the *Business Monitors* series (MQ6 and MA6) (IPS annually).

The English Tourist Board and the Welsh and Scottish Boards also conduct, together with the British Tourist Authority, annual visitor surveys and collect a wide range of information on the tourism market, primarily through the jointly sponsored British Home Tourism survey and the British National Survey. In the private sector the British Market Research Bureau (BMRB) carry out tourism surveys, but the results of these are only available to their clients or subscribers. Similarly the Henley Centre for forecasting produces a quarterly publication called *Leisure Futures* which includes trends and forecasts in patterns of tourism (Henley).

Using and measuring tourism data: Although a wide range of both aggregated and disaggregated data exists on international tourism in the developed countries, this information must be used with care, especially when making comparisons between countries. For example, the OECD data which is collected for 19 countries has almost as many different methods of measuring tourist flows. Thus Austria and Belgium have records from all registered tourist accommodation; Finland records hotel registrations only; while the Netherlands have records for hotels, motels and inns, but not self-catering or other forms of accommodation. Some countries such as the UK and France, base their estimates on frontier checks, supplemented by other surveys such as IPS in the UK. However, it is possible to provide a picture of overall trends in tourism and to determine the order of magnitude of tourist activity. Thus, even for Europe which has been collecting statistics on tourism for over 30 years, there is no common standard or agreed source for tourism data.

There is a great shortage of data on domestic tourism, and the annual reports of the OECD on *Tourism Policy and International Tourism* (OECD) indicate that among the member countries only the United States, Canada and the UK carry out annual surveys of their domestic tourist market. Most of the remaining countries either carry out periodic market research, directed at either the domestic industry or their major foreign markets, or sectoral studies of the tourist industry, usually on a one-off basis. The limitations of data on domestic tourism are particularly significant when we consider that about 90 per cent of world tourism is domestic tourism.

The purpose, scope and function of this book

As tourism does not appear on the GCE 'O' or 'A' level curriculum, most HND or degree students will be dealing with this subject for the first time. The overall aim of this book is to provide a broad foundation course in tourism studies. It is intended to provide an overview of the operations and characteristics of the tourist industry and the role of the private and public sectors in developing tourism. It is largely based on examples drawn from British experience, although where possible, material from a range of international sources is used, because tourism is essentially a world-wide phenomenon.

In order to provide a sound base of understanding tourism it is not sufficient to concentrate solely on business skills in the private sector or on planning and administration in the public sector. For this reason this book does not focus on such specific disciplines as business studies, law, geography, economics or management: such subject areas play a supporting role. The focus is on tourism. Its purpose is to highlight the interactions between the different sectors of the tourist industry and between components of the product consumed by tourists.

The remainder of this book focuses, therefore, on:

a) the study of tourism and its social, economic and environmental components;

b) providing an understanding of the operation of the private and public sectors and the interactions between them;

c) the behavioural aspects of tourism — tourists' motivations, perceptions and group characteristics.

ASSIGNMENTS

(i) Using visitor surveys, reports and annual statistics investigate the changes in the patterns of international and domestic tourism between 1974 and 1988, as they affect the UK.

(ii) You are employed by a national tourism office to produce a 750 word entry into a national tourism periodical. The task will, therefore, require you to consider the following:

(a) main resorts/visitor attractions;

(b) transport provision;

(c) amenity/entertainment;

(d) assessment of market;

(e) other factors, including climate.

You will be assessed according to the effectiveness of the 'copy' that you produce.

Chapter 2

The Development of the Tourist Industry

Learning Objectives: After reading this chapter and some of the references contained within it, you should understand how the industry has grown and developed; the form that the early tourist industry took; and the trends in travel and tourism in Britain since 1945.

Introduction

Throughout the ages man has travelled in search of new places, new lands, new cultures and experiences. History offers many examples, from Greek and Roman literature to Marco Polo, or Chaucer's pilgrims who were familiar with the famous shrines of Europe. For hundreds of years travel for the sake of pleasure was the prerogative of the rich because those who travelled needed an income to free their time for such purposes. For the majority of the population of Britain and Europe the feast days of the Church, i.e. holy-days, were their only break from work. Only those who were educated and prosperous and aware of foreign places engaged in such travel. It was only through trade or wars that most people visited distant places. Maps were crude or non-existent. Roads were bad, and risks abounded. Even in the late nineteenth century Robert Louis Stephenson commented on travelling in central France:

'A traveller of my sort was a thing hitherto unheard of in that district. I was looked on with contempt, like a man who should project a journey to the moon, yet with a respectful interest, like one setting forth for the inclement Pole.'

The Development of Mass Tourism

What changed this pattern? How did tourism, once the exclusive activity of the rich and well to-do, become an accepted part of life for the ordinary man and woman? To find the answer to these questions we must consider the requirements for travel and tourism. First, people must have the free time available and second, they must have the disposable income to spend. Thirdly, travel must be safe, reliable and relatively cheap. There must be attractions which travellers know of and which they wish to visit, and a range of amenities, especially accommodation, must be available. All of these conditions need to exist if mass tourism is to develop.

The Industrial Revolution from the mid-eighteenth century was the catalyst which brought all these conditions into being. Scientific inventions, new industrial processes, and new methods of production of manufactured goods changed society, first in Britain and then in America and Europe. An agricultural revolution formed part of this dynamic change improving the productivity of crops and animal husbandry and providing new wealth for industrial development. With the development of the steam engine and coal as a source of power, new maufacturing districts grew up on the coalfields of the north and midlands of England and central Scotland. The application of coal and coke to smelting iron and later steel accelerated this process. The reduction in the death rate through medical and public health improvements led to a steady growth in the population of England and Wales, from 5½ millions in 1702 to 9 millions in 1801.

The growth of Spas as Resort Towns

During the eighteenth century spa towns in England developed as places of resort for the rich and well to do, their seal of approval usually being a Royal visit. Conventional medicine vouched for the curative properties of their mineral waters, which though brackish and often foul-smelling, were drunk as well as bathed in. Bath is the best known of these with a reputation dating from Roman times.

The visits to Bath by King William in 1695 and Queen Anne in 1702 and 1703 set the seal on this as a fashionable place of resort. The town hired Beau Nash in 1705 to provide a range of entertainments during the 'season', although he also ensured that the city developed good roads, good accommodation for the visitor and set an example that many other towns were to copy. The medicinal reputation of the mineral waters was of prime importance for would-be spas and the distribution of mineral springs was therefore the earliest locational influence on these centres. Thus Scarborough developed as a spa town from 1627 (Lennard, 1931), and it was not until much later that its seaside location was to influence its long-term development as a resort.

The growth and spread of wealth among society encouraged more people to follow the fashion for taking mineral waters. By the mid-eighteenth century there were many spas, often of a purely local reputation, ranging from Bath at the height of fashion and the social scene, to Buxton, Leamington, Tunbridge Wells, Malvern and Gilsland. Epsom in fact came into being as a spa, and thereafter developed as a venue for horse racing with the Derby and the Oaks. By 1733 it was reported that the season at Scarborough had attracted almost one thousand of the nobility and the gentry. (Smollett, *Humphrey Clinker*). It was clear that by the mid-eighteenth century the now fashionable nature of this 'season' was an indication that the function of the larger spa towns was changing from that of a purely health resort to an important social centre where the leisured classes could spend their time.

During the second part of the eighteenth century there was a growth in small seaside 'watering places'. Sea bathing is depicted in an engraving of the South Bay, Scarborough (1735) and this print is the earliest record of bathing machines being used. In the seventeenth century sea bathing was recommended for gout and the medicinal value of sea water was given an added impetus by the publication of a *Dissertation concerning the Uses of Sea Water in Diseases of the Glands* by Dr Russel in 1753. The learned doctor also lived in Brighton and his advocacy of the virtues of sea water no doubt encouraged the growth of that resort. The arrival of the Prince of Wales in 1784 accelerated the growth of the town as a fashionable resort, just as royal visits to Bath had some eighty years earlier. In 1760 Brighton consisted of a large village with a population of 2,000. By 1820 it had over three thousand houses, a population of over 24,000 and more than 10,000 visitors a

Figure 4: Sketch diagram of a typical seaside resort

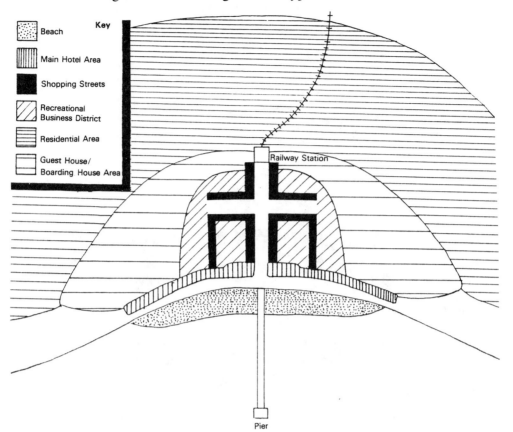

Key

- Beach
- Main Hotel Area
- Shopping Streets
- Recreational Business District
- Residential Area
- Guest House/Boarding House Area

Railway Station

Pier

year. During the late-eighteenth century many other coastal towns realised the potential of their seaside location and Lewis' *Topographical Dictionary* of 1835 lists dozens of former hamlets and small fishing villages, from Bognor Regis to Rhyl, that were transformed as seaside watering places.

Travel was still restricted to coach or horseback and most of these resorts were one or two days' journey from the major towns and cities. They were still resorts for a very limited section of society. To most of the working population they were remote and unknown places. The development of paddle steamers on the Thames in the early nineteenth century made the Kent coast resorts easily accessible to London for the first time. Almost 100,000 people were landed from London steamers on Margate pier in 1830. (Patmore, 1972).

The diffusion of wealth from the industrial and agricultural revolution brought more spending power to more of the population. In Britain the enclosure of agricultural land, and the growth of industrial towns, saw a mass migration from the countryside to the cities. At the end of the eighteenth century the population of England and Wales was 9 million. In 1851 it was 22 million and by 1901 had grown to 38 million. During this period the system of production changed from hand crafts to machine crafts; from small into large factories with the workers housed in nearby housing developments; and by the mid-nineteenth century over half of the population lived in the major towns.

Figure: 5 Origin of Visitors Resident in Keswick August Bank Holiday Week 1877

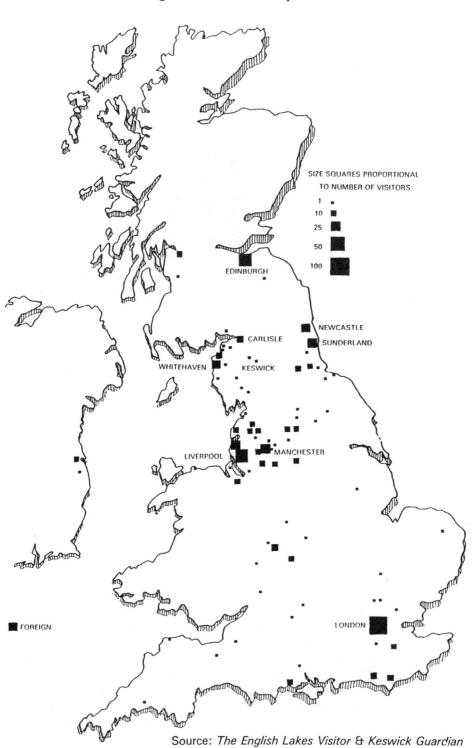

Source: *The English Lakes Visitor & Keswick Guardian*

The growth of seaside resorts in Victorian England

The transport system was transformed by the invention of the railway and its spread throughout Britain between 1832 and 1870. For the first time, fast, cheap and readily accessible passenger transport was available to most of the country's population. Enterprising developers and railway companies promoted links between the growing industrial cities and the coastal resorts, and with improved accessibility these prospered and rapidly grew in size. For example, the London, Tilbury and Southend Railway was opened and the population of the resort grew from 4,000 to 20,000 in 1901. Its present day population is over 150,000 and it receives over 6 million visitors a year, many of them still day trippers from London. The same pattern occurred at Brighton, Southport, Blackpool and many other, now familiar, coastal resorts. For example Brighton's population grew from 24,000 in 1820 to 99,000 in 1881 with the most rapid growth following the opening of the main London to Brighton line in 1841.

For the Victorian masses day excursions were the norm, rather than long holidays, although the diffusion of wealth and the growth of a middle class anxious to escape for a time from the industrial towns and cities introduced a wider spectrum of people to these resorts. This in turn led to a wider range of accommodation and amenities being offered.

Similarly in Europe once the railways linked the expanding industrial cities with the Mediterranean coast of France and Italy the select resorts of the upper classes were newly discovered by the growing middle classes anxious to emulate aristocratic fashions. In 1865 the railway arrived at Nice and two years later at Menton (Burnet, 1963) leading, in the period from 1865 to 1914, to the appearance of a number of thriving resorts along the Riviera coast which transformed it into the premier holiday region of France.

Some resorts had originally developed piers to accommodate visitors arriving by paddle steamer, but the practice of taking the sea air for health and relaxation, encouraged many resorts to build one if not more piers. The form and layout of most seaside resorts reflects both their development during the railway age and the strong attraction of the sea front. Most expanded parallel to the sea front with relatively little development inland. The main beach or promenade took over and copied the earlier spa promenade replacing the pump room as a focus of social life. Having arrived by train for a day visit or longer stay, the resort was the self contained provider of all the visitor's needs from accommodation to entertainment. Most of the land and buildings associated with the tourism industry are located in a zone between the railway station and the sea front with the prime frontal locations usually occupied in almost unbroken succession by the larger hotels. This pattern still persists today.

During the period between 1740 and 1840 the Lake District had been 'discovered' and due largely to the accounts of eighteenth century travellers and poets an appreciation of the 'wild' scenery of the area became fashionable. Within Britain it was in the Lake District more than anywhere else that the idea of a touring holiday developed. As early as 1793 it was reported that the number of 'strangers making the tour of the Lakes' who frequented Keswick, 'amounted to no less than 1,540'. (Brittain, 1802).

On the 5th July 1841 Thomas Cook organised his first rail excursion for one shilling return and by the 1870s all the railway companies ran regular cheap day excursions to the seaside. In 1871 the Bank Holiday Act provided four public holidays a year and after this date the extended family holiday at the seaside became more common.

The early attraction of the Alpine resorts as part of the eighteenth century Grand Tour, and the growth of winter sports and mountaineering in the late nineteenth century led to the spread of winter sports resorts in the Alpine districts of France, Switzerland, Italy and Austria. (Defert, 1958).

The appearance of a large middle class with the Industrial Revolution in Britain also provided a supply of potential tourists who were predominant in nineteenth century Europe. Cross channel traffic increased from 100,000 per annum in the 1830s to over 500,000 per annum in the 1890s. The major tourist countries of Europe had an unprecedented boom in the 1920s when France, Switzerland and Italy each received well over 1 million visitors (Lickorish, 1958). By 1930 over 1,500,000 British travelled to the Continent.

Mass Tourism

At the beginning of this chapter time and money were mentioned as constraints on participation in tourism. By the beginning of the twentieth century most people still had limited opportunities for tourism and the factory system allowed few days off outside the statutory holidays.

During the 1920s and 1930s holidays with pay became more common and in 1925 the Ministry of Labour estimated that 1½ million manual workers received holidays with pay. In 1938 the *Holidays with Pay Act* gave a new stimulus to mass tourism, and by June 1939 over 11 million workers received holidays with pay (Brunner, 1945) and almost one person in three went away from home for a holiday. By 1945 80 per cent of the workforce received holidays with pay. (Patmore, 1972).

New types of holiday were developed in inter-war Britain among them camping and youth hostelling. Membership of the YHA rose from 6,439 in 1931 to 83,418 in 1939. The membership of the Camping Club of Great Britain rose from 3,000 in 1933 to 7,000 in 1935. In 1937 Billy Butlin promoted the first holiday camp at Skegness and by 1939 there were 200 such camps scattered around the coasts of Britain catering for 30,000 holidaymakers a week during the season. (Brunner, 1945). Thus during the 1930s through the holidays with pay movement, tourism no longer remained the preserve of the rich and well-to-do. It became an accepted activity for the majority of Britain's population.

The years following the Second World War saw a gradual growth in tourist activity. The geographic scale of the War had broken down international barriers and introduced great social changes. Those returning from the War expected greater opportunities, better living standards and more activity in their lives. This was to affect the scale of both domestic and international tourism.

Post-1945 Domestic Tourism

There was no sudden dramatic change in the pattern of domestic tourism, although the numbers spending a holiday away from home continued to grow as the population of Britain grew and more of the workforce had holidays with pay.

There was little change in the pattern of tourist destinations. More than two thirds of all main holidays were taken at the seaside. Holiday camps were replacing the traditional resort as a basis for a self-contained 'package' catering for all the visitors' needs. Billy Butlin pioneered the first such camp at Skegness in 1937 and by 1939 there were 200 such camps around the British coast catering for 30,000 people a week. Public transport was still popular in 1951 and only 25 per cent travelled by car. The Festival of Britain in 1951 and the Coronation of Elizabeth the Second in 1953 gave an impetus to the development of new tourist facilities. The Government introduced a limited grant scheme to provide financial help (albeit limited) to hotels catering for overseas visitors and in the 1956 *Distribution of Industry Act,* which gave the Treasury powers to make loans or grants in areas of high unemployment, hotels were included for the first time. It was during this

Figure 6: Overseas visitors to United Kingdom 1945—1970

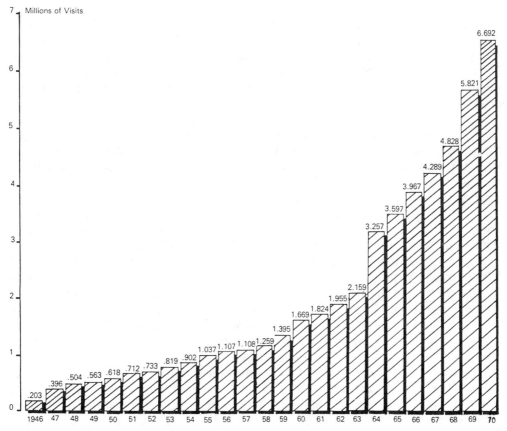

period of the mid to late 1950s that the then British Travel Association attempted to encourage holidays in Britain with a cooperative scheme in which the British resorts and industry took part. This was designed to extend the holiday season and to encourage more people to visit Britain's holiday resorts.

The number of visitors to Britain from overseas also grew rapidly during the 1950s from 203,000 in 1946 to 1.7 million in 1960. Initially 69 per cent of these foreign visitors arrived by sea and 31 per cent by air. But the dramatic growth in air travel during the 1960s reversed these figures. From the development of holidays with pay in the 1930s to the growth of overseas visitors during the 1950s and 1960s the domestic tourist industry came of age. Within the space of thirty years there emerged a major industry employing hundreds of thousands of people and producing many millions of pounds for the national economy. It is a very large and complex industry often with linkages between hotel groups, travel companies, transport operators, promotional agencies and tourist boards.

Foreign Tourism

Until the late 1950s the bulk of the British took their main holiday in the UK, often at a seaside resort, and usually during July and August. There had been little change in the nature of the holiday destination for over 100 years. In 1951 only 1½ million out of a total population of 50 million Britons chose to go abroad for their holidays, (British Travel Association, 1970) spending £60 million in the process.

By 1970 5¾ million Britons took their holidays abroad spending £470 million. Over 25 per cent of these holidaymakers were aged between 16 and 24. In 1950 France was the most popular holiday destination attracting 40 per cent of the Britons taking foreign holidays. The most dramatic change during this period was the tremendous growth in the popularity of Spain. Of the 5.75 million Britons taking foreign holidays in 1970 nearly one-third went to Spain.

What brought about this dramatic growth in foreign holidays? The immediate post war years were a period when there were many surplus aircraft and highly trained aircrews who wished to continue flying in civilian life.

Technological improvements in aircraft and engine design during the 1950s helped to reduce the relative cost of air travel. The cost of travel to a foreign country is a key element in its attractiveness as a holiday destination, together with the level of accommodation and general living costs that exist there. Between 1950 and 1968 (see Table 2)the cost of a high season return from London to New York almost halved in price and almost every route operated showed a marked reduction in the cost of air travel during this 18-year period.

To have the means to travel is not enough. There need to be enough air services between the tourist generating countries (such as Britain) and the tourist receiving countries (such as Spain or Italy) to meet the peak season travel demands. Two trends emerged during this period. First average aircraft seating capacity almost doubled (Table 3) for intra-European flights and almost trebled for transatlantic routes. Second, in Britain private airline companies were allowed by the Government to develop and to set up in competititon with the State airlines. By the early 1960s the potential airline traveller to Spain or Greece, for example, could travel as an independent passenger on a scheduled or chartered flight as part of an inclusive group tour, or as an inclusive tour passenger on a scheduled flight in the mid and late 1950s.

It was the development of chartered flights which transformed the pattern of annual holidays for millions of British tourists. Foreign travel, for so long the prerogative of the rich, became easily accessible to the general population. In the early 1950s tour operators began to market package tours to the Continent linking up with private airlines such as Laker Airways and, by the early 1960s, Spain and the Mediterranean were being promoted and developed as holiday destinations for millions of Britons. The tour operators for the first time put together a foreign holiday 'package' covering travel, accommodation, meals and sometimes other items at an inclusive price. By chartering aircraft and filling every seat the operator could keep travel costs down and, by making block bookings in particular hotels, could also provide accommodation at competitive prices. During the 1960s extensive tracts of the Costa Brava and Costa Blanca in Spain, and in the 1970s the Languedoc-Rousillon coast, were developed to meet this tourist boom. Today there are many kinds of holiday package and as many different holiday destinations. The sun, sea and sand package of the summer months is replaced by the sun, snow and skiing package over the Christmas — winter period.

Throughout the 1960s to the 1980s individual income levels continued to grow and levels of car ownership in Britain grew from 2 million in 1950 to 17.7 million in 1981. By 1980 39 per cent of overseas travel to Western Europe used the Channel ferries — much of this traffic being private cars. The escalation in petrol prices following the 1973 Arab-Israeli conflict caused a temporary downturn in this trend, but by the early 1980s the number of Britons taking their cars on Continental holidays was again increasing. The development of motorway links to the Channel ports in Britain and similar improvements on the autoroutes in France, Belgium and Holland brought many more European resorts within driving distance from Britain, and this too — together with the easing of EEC frontier controls — made foreign travel much easier and attractive.

Even the recession from the late 1970s has failed to halt the demand for foreign holidays. In 1982, despite massive growth in unemployment, 8 per cent more Britons travelled abroad and spent 20 per cent more. (TAC *Anatomy of UK Tourism*).

In Britain the Government took the first steps to a national policy for tourism with the *Development of Tourism Act* in 1969. It established a British Tourist Authority, English, Scottish and Wales Tourist Boards with powers to provide loans and grants for hotel development schemes; to encourage the provision and improvement of tourist amenities and facilities; and to promote Britain as a tourist destination for overseas visitors. The results of this Act and the development of public sector tourism in Britain are discussed at greater length in Chapter 8. Its importance in this context is that by the 1970s the Government recognised the growing importance of the tourist industry both as an employer of labour and as a major contributor to the national economy.

Other trends in tourism are beginning to emerge as new fashions and new holiday concepts appear. Time-sharing, villa holidays, Club 18 to 30, golfing holidays, trips to China, India or the West Indies, all highlight the importance of travel in our lives and the inventiveness of companies to develop and market new types of holiday product. These developments are discussed in Chapter 13.

ASSIGNMENT

On the basis of tourist data showing trends in domestic and international tourism 1950 to 1980, provide a summary of the main changes which have taken place during this period, and outline the underlying causes of these changes.

Chapter 3

The Structure of the Tourist Industry in Britain

Learning Objectives: After reading this Chapter you should understand the nature of and linkages between the different sectors of the tourist industry, and its importance to the national economy.

Introduction

The demand for tourism which has grown steadily over the past 40 years is a demand for a bundle of goods and services and these are provided by both the private and public sectors of the national economy. The private sector provides much of the accommodation and visitor attractions, the public sector provides much of the existing infrastructure especially the transport facilities. Within the tourist industry there is a great degree of interdependence between the private and public sectors and the structure of the industry clearly reflects this characteristic.

The tourist industry in Britain directly employs over one million people, and earns over £6,000 million a year from spending by overseas visitors. Within Britain the industry is geared to two ends. First, meeting the needs of incoming tourists and Britons taking a holiday within the United Kingdom (Domestic Tourism); and secondly meeting the needs of British holidaymakers seeking foreign holidays. (Outgoing Tourism).

The Tourism Product

The tourist product is the resort or historic town, the beaches, scenery, mountains, historic sites, theme parks, museums and other similar tourist attractions. It is also the stock of accommodation that caters for the needs of the tourist. The difference between the tourist industry and other industries is that the tourist goods and services unlike other goods and services are not transported to their users but instead the consumers are transported to where the tourist product exists and production and consumption take place there. The industry therefore consists of three main sectors:

1. Suppliers of Tourist Services, Facilities and Attractions

There are five main types of activity within this general classification. These include accommodation, restaurants and cafes, conference facilities, passenger transport, car hire, motoring organisations, and tourist attractions and entertainment. Between them these activities employ over 200,000 people with accommodation and catering being the dominant sectors. The firms involved in these activities are often small in size and usually private companies, although some of the tourist attractions and transport facilities are in the public or quasi-public sector.

The main occupations in the tourist services sector are:

Service staff in hotels and guest houses

These consist of waiters and waitresses, chambermaids, porters and bar staff and together they account for about 65,000 jobs in the UK domestic tourist industry. Traditionally much of this workforce is seasonal and there is a substantial movement between jobs. A survey by the Education Training Advisory Council in 1983 (ETAC 1983) of the industry estimated that between 1983 and 1987 some 200,000 managers, supervisors and crafts people would be needed to meet the growth in jobs and loss of people from this sector of the industry.

Managers in hotels

There are about 50,000 general managers throughout the UK, many being working owners of small hotels and guest houses. Of these about 7,000 are front of house or specialist managers, generally employed by the larger hotel chains.

The accommodation sector has been expanding steadily over the past 15 years, in line with the development of the tourist industry and the increase in conference business in the main resorts. (Chapter 7 examines this sector in more detail).

Travel agency staff

Counter and reservations staff in travel agencies are mainly employed by high street retail travel agencies, and this sector of the market is growing as some companies such as Thomas Cook and Pickfords increase the number of their high street branches. Currently about 14,000 people are employed in this sector. In addition about 2,000 to 2,500 management jobs exist in the travel agency/tour operations business in the UK.

There are over 50,000 people working in a wide variety of tourist attractions ranging from seaside amusement arcades and shows to stately homes, museums and galleries and theme parks. Some of these, especially those located in seaside resorts, are seasonal whilst others may be open all year attracting local people on day or half-day visits as well as touring visitors.

2.   Travel Operations Staff

This covers British Rail, the cross-Channel ferry operators and the airlines who deal with both domestic tourism and outgoing tourism. The airlines experienced a period of steady expansion during the 1960s and 1970s reflecting the overall growth in tourists travelling by air and the increasing use of air charters especially from the regional airports. The British airlines and overseas carriers employ over 4,000 managers in the UK and overall about 60,000 people are employed by the major airlines.

The ferry operations also saw a growth in traffic during this period and in the late 1970s some newcomers came on the scene such as Sally Lines (from Ramsgate) and Olau Line (from Sheerness).

About 10,000 people are employed in the passenger management services with about 4,000 stewards and attendants.

About 6,000 people are involved in coach tour operations, mainly in small firms with less than 30 employees. De-regulation of the coach industry in the autumn of 1986 has provided new opportunities for expansion of coach touring and opened up more routes for competition. (Chapter 6 provides an overview of recent developments in the passenger transport sector).

3. Destination Management and Administration

It is an interesting aspect of the tourist industry in that although it consists mainly of private sector firms and organisations, much of the promotional work for the tourist destinations within the UK is done by public sector bodies. In 1969 following the *Development of Tourism Act* a British Tourist Authority was established together with 3 boards responsible for England, Scotland and Wales. (This Act and subsequent developments are discussed more fully in Chapter 8). There has also been a growth in tourism promotion at local authority level and not only in the main seaside resorts. Many towns in holiday areas now operate tourist information centres and have an interest in tourism because of its job creation potential. There are now over 1,000 staff in management positions in these organisations. In addition there are now over 700 Tourist Information Centres (TICs) in the UK and over 1,000 people are employed in clerical and administrative jobs in this sector of the industry.

Very often the destination organisation (especially the National and Regional Tourist Boards) will have commercial members who provide an important source of revenue income supplementing that received directly from central government. Some of these commercial members will be board members, giving the private sector a voice in the development of public sector tourism policies. The publication of *Pleasure, Leisure and Jobs — the business of tourism,* in 1985 underlined the government's desire to improve opportunities for development of tourism, particularly for small businesses. This commitment to tourism development was underlined in 1987 by the publication of the English Tourist Board's 5-year development plan *A Vision For England.*

Trade/professional organisations

A variety of organisations have evolved to represent the many different interests which make up the tourist industry. They are mainly organised on a sectoral basis, for example the Hotel, Catering and Institutional Management Association (HCIMA), the British Hotels Restaurants and Caterers Association, The Chartered Institute of Transport (CIT), the Institute of Travel and Tourism (ITT) and the Association of British Travel Agents (ABTA). In some tourist regions groups of tourist attractions have combined forces to market their product. For example, in Cornwall 24 centres have formed the Cornwall association of tourist attractions. The general aims of these bodies is to represent the particular interests of their members, to promote certain standards of service and to act as a lobby to government. Some professional organisations such as the HCIMA (The Hotel, Catering and Institutional Management Association), ABTA (The Association of British Travel Agents), and the ITT (The Institute of Travel and Tourism) are concerned about education and training for the industry and the provision of a suitable range of courses to meet the industry's needs. Other groups often referred to in the trade press are BITOA (British Incoming Tour Operators Association) the ATUC (The Air Transport Users Committee), CAA (Civil Aviation Authority) and the TOSG (Tour Operators Study Group).

However, each of these bodies represents an individual sector, and no single organisation exists to speak for the interests of the industry as a whole. Even the professional associations are mainly concerned with relatively narrow needs. Thus ABTA is concerned about training for travel agency/tour operations work, HCIMA with catering and hotel or institutional management. There is a clear need for an overall body to integrate the industry and present a single voice to central government and with a unified view of the education and training needs of the industry.

The Domestic Tourist Industry

This consists of two elements:-

(i)   *Tourism arrivals in Britain:* In 1987 over 15 million overseas tourists came to Britain spending over £6 billion. Between 1975 and 1987 the level of spending by foreign tourists to Britain increased from £1,225 million to over £6,000 million.

(ii)   *Holidays by the British within their own country:* In 1988 they made 156 million visits, spent 505 million nights away from home and their total spending was over £7,800 million.

These two elements of the domestic market have quite different holiday preferences and patterns of behaviour and for this reason are discussed separately. For example, the greatest proportion of overseas visitors came to London and South East England and Scotland whilst the West country which is the major destination for British holiday-makers, receives less than 10 per cent of overseas visitors.

Overseas Tourists

In 1988, 57% of overseas visitors came from Western Europe, a further 23% from North America and the remainder mainly from Africa and Australasia.

The main gateways for overseas visitors are the Channel ports of Dover and Folkestone and the two airports close to London — Gatwick and Heathrow. The concentration of these gateways around London helps to enhance its position as Britain's main tourist destination for overseas visitors. In 1988 9.2 million overseas visitors spent part of their stay in London and 14 million Britons had

Figure 7: DESTINATION OF TOURISM IN ENGLAND
(British Residents Only)

NORTHUMBRIA
5

CUMBRIA
4

YORKSHIRE &
HUMBERSIDE
10

NORTH
WEST
9

EAST MIDLANDS
8

WALES

HEART
OF
ENGLAND
10

ENGLAND

EAST ANGLIA
10

THAMES &
CHILTERNS
7

LONDON
12

SOUTHERN
9

SOUTH EAST
12

WEST COUNTRY
17

Source: British Tourist Authority 1988

British Tourism Survey Monthly

Note: Visits to the
regions will add to more
than the total as some
visitors visited more than
one region.

Figure Millions of British Tourist
visits to the Tourist Board
Regions (1988)

Total British Tourist Trips
= 145m trips (1980)
(11% of these went abroad)

holidays in the city. Together they produced an income of £3,895 millions and tourism generated an estimated one in ten jobs in Greater London.

The overseas visitors and British visitors complement each other. Thus the overseas visitors concentrate on London and several historic towns and cities, whereas the British holidaymakers still prefer seaside holidays.

Outside of London and the South East, Scotland attracts more overseas visitors than any other tourist region, particularly North American tourists who account for about 40 per cent of overseas visitors to Scotland. The typical overseas tourist will aim to visit several major cities and about one-third of foreign tourists come on inclusive tours. A typical tour will include 3 or 4 days in London with a 'milk run' which takes in Bath, Stratford on Avon, Chester, the Lake District, Edinburgh and York or Cambridge returning again to London.

About half of overseas visitors are tourists on holiday, about one-fifth are on business and one-fifth visiting friends and relatives. Six out of ten arrive by air — a proportion that has remained very stable over the past decade.

The bulk of overseas visitors arrive between July and September, and this seasonal peaking together with a concentration of visits in London and several historic towns and cities presents a planning problem for the national and regional tourist boards who promote Britain as a tourist destination.

There is a need to market the 'shoulder months' and to promote new venues/new locations for overseas visitors, with the aim of relieving peak season pressure on London's tourist resources, spreading the benefits of overseas visitor income to the local economy, and increasing the overall numbers of overseas visitors to Britain.

The British Tourist Authority promotes tourism to Britain from most overseas countries and concentrates in particular on target marketing and promotional efforts such as the youth market, the senior citizen market and special interest markets. The BTA generally uses cooperative promotions with all sections of the tourist industry involved in the marketing of Britain. This includes airlines, ships, rail, travel agents, tour operators, car hire companies, hotel groups and so on. The BTA also promotes a campaign to attract tourists over the shoulder months with its 'operation off peak', and this approach is discussed in more detail in Chapter 10 which deals with the marketing of travel and tourism.

Outgoing Tourism

In 1988 over 26 million Britons took overseas holidays, with France (25 per cent) and Spain (20 per cent) as the main destinations (Department of Trade and Industry figures). The number of outgoing tourists increased by 1 million over the 1987 figures, largely due to an intensive marketing campaign by all the major tour operators during the winter and spring of 1987. As 55% of all UK residents taking foreign holidays (excluding the Irish Republic) do so on an inclusive tour, such a campaign can have an immediate effect on outgoing tourism. The inclusive tour market largely concentrates on package holidays to Spain (38% of all inclusive tours), France (14%), Greece (8%), and Italy (8%).

Most people buying package holidays (i.e. a return flight and accommodation either in an hotel, or self catering) will do so from a high street travel agent who represents the retail side of the travel trade. Some may offer special interest packages such as golfing holidays or fly-drive packages, to suit the needs of particular market segments. Whilst the *travel agent* will *sell* the package or 'inclusive tour' as it is known in the industry, it is the *tour operator* who will usually put the package together, negotiating arrangements with air or sea and land carriers, hotel groups and other resort services, and selling the package at a single price to the retail travel agent. At present in Britain there are around 7,000 high street Travel Agency outlets and about 6 major tour operators. The complex nature of the mass travel market is outlined more fully in Chapter 5.

Distribution of the Tourist Industry in Britain

If the tourist product is the resort or historic town or an amalgam of natural or man-made attractions, it follows that the industry which services this product will be concentrated in quite specific locations which are associated with it. From the large, brash seaside resorts such as Blackpool or Brighton to the quiet inland villages such as Grasmere or Bourton on the Water, they all have one feature in common — a large part of their economy is bound up with catering for and entertaining visitors.

Resorts in general are peripheral — both in Britain and Western Europe and most have a coastal location. The popularity of seaside holidays in Britain; 80 per cent in Spain) has long established the pre-eminence of coastal towns as centres of the tourist industry. In Western Europe (including Britain) over 90 per cent of resorts have a coastal location. Added to these are two other types of resort — the capital cities such as London, Paris or Rome whose position as centres of government, business and culture make them major attractions in their own right, and secondly towns with historic cultural associations such as Stratford, or York, Heidleberg, or Oxford.

The traditional resort town shows a pattern of land use that is often centred on the 'resort' function of the town. Thus the traditional seaside resort shows a pattern of land use, shape and layout that is repeated world-wide. Buildings with a tourism function and the associated infrastructure of the resort are often concentrated in a relatively narrow sector of the town, such as along the coastal/beach-front strip — particularly opposite the main pier/amusement part or casino — with a gradual decline in tourist activity away from the main foci of interest. Most seaside resorts expanded parallel to the sea-front with relatively little development inland — a pattern repeated from Blackpool to Ocean City.

The townscape of most resorts reflects their history of rapid development with a great influx of capital investment in the form of hotels, entertainment complexes, amusement parks, promenades and piers — all of which are so familiar to us today.

In Britain most resorts were well established by the late nineteenth century. For most tourists up to the 1960s the most popular form of travel was by rail, and having arrived by train the resort was a self-contained provider of all the visitor's needs from accommodation to entertainment because the tourist was not mobile and spent most of his holiday within the resort. This is reflected in the layout of the seaside resorts, with the railway station, the main shopping and tourist streets leading to or along the sea-front, which usually had a promenade and pier. Along this sea-front area are grouped the hotels and boarding houses, shops and entertainment areas.

Figure 8 : A Typical 'Milk Run' For Overseas Visitors

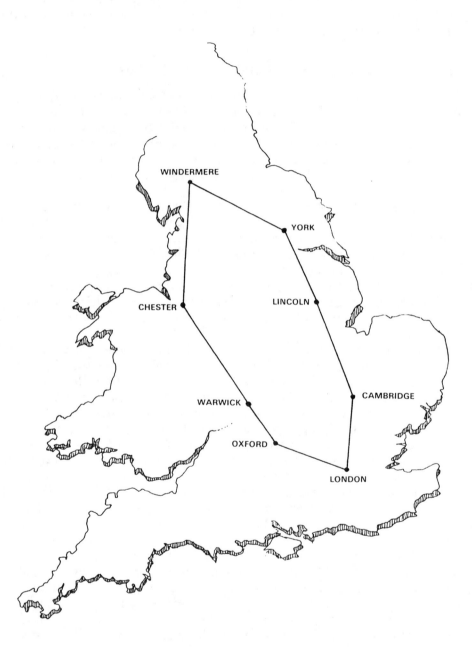

Although this range of land uses persists, the types of tourist and the patterns of tourism are quite different to those who contributed to the original growth and wealth of resorts in Britain. Today's tourist, if they are from overseas, will be visiting several resorts perhaps staying a short time in each and will be highly mobile. Most domestic holidaymakers arrive by car and more often tend to use resorts for short break holidays in spring or autumn as a supplement to an annual holiday abroad. They have quite different wants and objectives compared with their predecessors. They are much more mobile — most arrive by car, much more curious about the surrounding area, and more affluent and discriminating. Seaside resorts have had to adapt to this new kind of tourist, and to more fierce competition from abroad or alternative forms of tourist destination. For example, groups of resorts and formed consortia to market their product more effectively and one of the best known of these is the Torbay area which uses the slogan 'The English Riviera'.

New types of tourist destination have also emerged. Some are industrial towns that have cleverly packaged their surrounding hinterland often exploiting historical or literary associations. For example, Bradford stresses its links with the Bronte sisters, whilst South Tyneside promotes itself as 'Catherine Cookson Country'. Other attractions are based on Britain's rich and pioneering industrial heritage such as the Ironbridge Museum at Coalbrookdale which traces the story of iron and steel-making, or the North of England Open Air Museum at Beamish. The Beamish Museum, which covers over 300 acres has recreated a microcosm of industrial life in North-East England as it was in the early years of the 20th century.

Since their creation in the late 1940s the 10 national parks of England and Wales have attracted growing numbers of tourists — although they often contained long-established resorts such as Keswick (Lake District), Buxton (Peak District) or Tenby (Pembrokeshire). More recently, some of the national parks have seen the growth of time-sharing developments — an issue discussed in more detail in Chapter 13.

Since the 1960s the UK seaside resorts have seen a decline in their share of the long stay holiday market due to the growth of competitive package holidays to the Mediterranean. One of the overriding issues facing many traditional resorts is that of adapting the resort amenities and infrastructure to meet the changing needs of tourists in the 1980s and beyond. The resort authorities need to identify development opportunities, they need to consider ways and means of increasing their share of the tourist market, of attracting commercial investment, and of promoting the resort development package. A key element in their development strategy is the provision of all-weather leisure attractions in the form of indoor resort complexes, such as the multi-million pound Sandcastle Development opened in Blackpool in 1986.

ASSIGNMENT

Using national census data for 1981 and 1971, look at the changing nature of tourism employment in Britain. What sectors of the industry have shown the greatest change? Why do you think this is?

DIRECT EMPLOYMENT SECTORS: PRINCIPAL ACTIVITIES

Principal sector	Activity* code	Constituent activities	Notes
Hotels and Catering	665	Hotel trade	excludes all
	661	Restaurant and cafes etc.	institutional catering and
	662	Public houses and bars	catering
	663	Night clubs and licensed clubs	linked with work
	667	Other tourist etc. accommodation	
Travel and transport services	710	Railways	
	721,772,726	Other inland transport	excluding road haulage
	740	Sea transport	
	750	Air transport	
		Transporting supporting services	
Tourism, leisure and entertainment facilities	969	Tourism and other services	
	914	Theatre, television, radio	
	977	Libraries, museums and galleries	
	979	Sports and other leisure services	

*As defined in the *Standard Industrial Classification,* 1980

Chapter 4

International Tourism : An Overview

Learning Objectives: After reading this chapter and the source material referred to, and tackling one of the assignments, you should understand the nature, scope and distribution of international tourism, the factors that influence its development and its importance in the world economy.

Introduction

Tourism is the largest industry in the world, and by any definition the most international activity. International Tourism, that is travel for holiday or pleasure from one country to another, is not a new phenomenon and can be traced back to Greek and Roman times. As the last chapter indicated international tourism grew rapidly through the nineteenth and early twentieth centuries, but in terms of sheer volume of tourists travelling abroad, it is a relatively recent phenomenon. Mass tourism is a post World War 2 development. This chapter seeks to give a brief account of recent trends in international tourism and its impact on the world's economy and it analyses the factors that have affected, and are likely to affect, the future expansion of international tourism.

Data Sources on International Tourism

The most comprehensive set of statistics on international tourism are published by the Organisation for Economic Cooperation and Development based in Paris. This organisation, which was established in 1960, represents most of the advanced industrial nations of the world and includes among its members all the European countries, the United States, Japan, New Zealand and Australia. The OECD publishes an annual report on *Tourism Policy and International Tourism in OECD Member Countries* and this contains a wide range of detailed returns on tourist flows and expenditures for all the OECD member states. The first half of this annual report includes a country by country update on government policy and action relating to tourism. Although this OECD data provides much valuable information on international tourist flows, it must be used carefully. Each member state makes a count of all foreign visitors as they enter this country and this is recorded under the 'arrivals'. If for example an English tourist is en route overland for Austria he could be recorded an 'arrival' in France, Germany and Switzerland before he reaches his main tourist destination, so it is important to treat 'arrivals' statistics with caution. Moreover, no checks are made on the purpose of the visit, and few countries collect detailed information on the international travel patterns of their own population.

Since 1966 the World Tourism Organisation has produced an *Annual Economic Review of World Tourism*. However, although this includes information on Africa, Asia and Oceania not contained in the OECD report, it does not have the sheer volume of detailed statistical data, and is much more of an annual overview of trends in the main regions of the world.

A further useful source is a US publication, the *Travel Industry World Yearbook : The Big Picture*. This publication, which appears annually, provides a very comprehensive overview of trends in World Tourism drawing on a wide range of national and international tourist statistics. Although biased towards the USA market, it brings together a valuable set of data on travel trends, economic and political influences and forecasts on the future prospects for world tourism.

The Economist Intelligence Unit publishes *International Tourism Quarterly,* renamed *International Tourism Reports* in 1986, which provides detailed country and regional profiles of tourism. EIU also publishes *Travel and Tourism Analyst* on a monthly basis, an invaluable source of data on international tourism developments.

One of the problems faced when dealing with international travel and tourism statistics is that there are great differences between international organisations and individual countries in the coverage and systems of data collection. The four main international organisations dealing with the collection of travel and tourism data are the United National Statistical Office (UNSO), the World Tourism Organisation (WTO), the International Civil Aviation Organisation (ICAO) and the International Air Transport Association (IATA). These four bodies use six different classifications for world tourism regions. The Department of Trade and Industry in the UK groups tourism origin and destination countries into four regions, whilst the US Travel and Tourism Administration uses nine regions worldwide. This variation in systems of regionalisation means that data on tourist flows within and between regions must be treated with caution.

Tourist Generating Countries

Although Tourism is now a world-wide phenomenon, the main tourist generating countries are concentrated in North America and Western Europe. Two countries in particular, West Germany and the United States account for about 40 per cent of tourist arrivals, and Europe and North America account for 83 per cent of the entire movement of international tourist arrivals. (WTO 1986). This pattern has remained fairly constant for the past 20 years, although Japan is now becoming more important as a tourist generating country. Table 4 on page 36 which is based on WTO and OECD statistics emphasises the predominance of the United States and Europe on the world scene.

The main tourist generating countries have five common characteristics. Their domestic population have the disposable income to spend on foreign holidays; they have a level of awareness of foreign countries, through literature, the media and promotional campaigns; the infrastructure exists to package, sell and organise foreign travel; they have the free time to take holidays, and lastly the geographical characteristics of these regions provide a variety of destinations that are in close proximity and accessible.

General Trends in International Tourism

In 1984 total international trips, including travel for holidays and leisure as well as for business and other special reasons were estimated at $300 million (WTO 1986) and total receipts from international travel were $100,000 million. The demand for international tourism (Figure 9) has increased steadily since 1960 and the total number of arrivals has grown more than four times over the past 27 years. However, although demand has grown dramatically, most of this has remained concentrated in Europe and North America. Despite this, the developing countries have increased their share of tourist arrivals every year. Some regions such as parts of North Africa, East Asia and the Pacific have shown above average growth in their share of tourist arrivals.

In the Americas over 2 million more tourists arrived between 1982 and 1984, but Central and South America and the Caribbean showed a greater overall growth in international arrivals. Most of the tourist traffic is generated by the USA and Canada, who accounted for example for 90% of arrivals in the Caribbean (WTO 1986). Because of the sheer size of the USA and Canada, and the vast distances involved in travelling to other countries, most of their domestic population prefer to take holidays within their own country. Similarly in Central and South America over 75% of arrivals are from within Latin America.

In the early 1980s Europe alone took up 70% of international tourist arrivals. The strength of Europe both as a generator and receiver of tourists is due to the following factors:

(i)   More than half of the population takes a period of paid holidays and leisure every year;

(ii)   European incomes are higher than incomes of many regions of the world and there is a comparable system of paid leave, flexible frontier controls, protection of tourists and a government commitment to tourism development;

(iii)   There is a large and well established tourist industry and infrastructure;

(iv)   There are a wealth of natural, cultural and historical attractions.

(v)   The geography of Europe means that distances between countries are relatively small: there is a comprehensive road, rail and air network which makes travel quick and easy; and Europeans are highly mobile.

Table 3
Changes in Average Aircraft Capacity 1954—66

Year	Transatlantic	European Routes
1954	54	46
1958	67	52
1962	128	70
1966	144	84

Source: IATA Annual Statistics

Table 4
International Tourist Receipts 1950—1984
(£ millions)

Region	1950	1960	1970	1984
Europe	318	1,399	3,250	57,650
N America	238	496	1,070)	
Latin America & Caribbean	140	372	780)	23,367
Middle East	9	32	132	4,000
Africa	32	63	121	2,150
Asia	13	82	252	13,200
TOTAL	750	2,444	6,575	100,000

Source: WTO

Within Europe, in the period between 1967 and 1987 there has been a redistribution of tourist demand, with Britain, Spain and Greece sharing the greatest growth income from international tourism. Between 1967 and 1981 the number of overseas visitors to Britain increased by 500% and to Greece by over 160%. For the same period Europe as a whole almost doubled its share of international tourism, taking $58,000 million in 1984 (WTO 1986). Eighty per cent of international travel in Europe is a result of intra-European travel. This is particularly the case in the main European tourist destinations, where intra-regional arrivals accounted for 91 per cent of international arrivals to Italy and 95 per cent in Spain. In 1987 Spain received over 51 million visitors with a revenue of over £7 million.

In Africa the recovery in travel to the Mediterranean coast of North Africa largely accounts for the growth in international tourism to the continent in the 1980s. This part of Northern Africa with its proximity to the main tourist generating countries of Europe and a long established tourism tradition accounts for over 60 per cent of international arrivals in Africa. The other main tourist region is West Africa, particularly Kenya and Zimbabwe which receive over 17 per cent of international arrivals (WTO 1986).

The growth of international tourism in Africa was encouraged by increased promotion and the development of inclusive tours designed to attract tourists from Europe and North America. Between 1977 and 1983 tourism receipts in Africa increased by over 9 per cent per year, with Southern Africa achieving the fastest growth with over 20 per cent per year (WTO 1986).

In East Asia and the Pacific there were over 26.5 million tourist arrivals in 1984 (WTO 1986). The main tourist destinations within the region are Singapore, Hong Kong, Fiji and Samoa. Table 5 on page 37 brings out the importance of tourism to the economies of these areas. Asia is the second most popular long-haul market for Europeans after the United States. In 1984 about 3.2 million Europeans travelled to Asia compared with 1.6 million to sub-Saharan Africa and 1 million to the Caribbean. Although there was growth in business travel from Europe to Hong Kong and Japan in the first half of the 1980s, there has only been a slight increase in leisure travel to this region. The weakening of the dollar — to which a

Table 5
International Tourist Receipts as a proportion of
national income for selected destinations

Place	International Tourist Receipts as a proportion of national income
	Per Cent
Singapore	16.0
Fiji	13.0
Samoa	12.5
Hong Kong	5.5

(By comparison UK = 1.2 per cent)

(Source: WTO Economic Review of World Tourism 1986)

number of Asian currencies are linked — will have an impact, and should encourage the growth of long haul trips in the late 1980s.

In Japan the domestic tourist industry is having to deal with the long term increase in the value of the yen against other international currencies, and arrivals figures in 1986 showed a continuing drop in the number of inland tourists. In contrast the Japanese outbound market is very strong, with over 6.5 million Japanese taking overseas holidays in 1987.

The economic significance of international tourism is best measured by comparing receipts with Gross Domestic Product (GDP) and expenditures with Private Final Consumption (PFC). Unfortunately, it is not possible to make detailed comparisons on a world scale because of the deficiencies in world economic data, and in this case the only detailed data exist for the OECD member states.

Table 6
International Travel Receipts 1984
(in millions of US dollars)

Region	International Travel Receipts	%
Africa	2,150	2.1
Americas	24,000	24.00
East Asia and the Pacific	11,000	11.00
Middle East	4,000	4.00
South Asia	1,200	1.2
Europe	57,650	57.6
World	100,000	100.00

(Source: WTO 1986)

Table 7 indicates the relative share of tourist activity in total economic activity for 1981. It shows that total receipts accounted for the greatest direct contribution to economic activity in France and Greece where they came to over 5 per cent of GDP and Germany and the United Kingdom (over 4 per cent of GDP).

Total tourist expenditures as a component of Private Final Consumption were most important in West Germany where they accounted for 10.5 per cent of PFC, and France (7.6%). This percentage was least significant in Greece (only 1% of PFC).

The contribution of tourism to economic activity is significantly greater than the estimates based on direct visitor spending would suggest. Tourist spending in a

Figure 9: International Tourism Demand

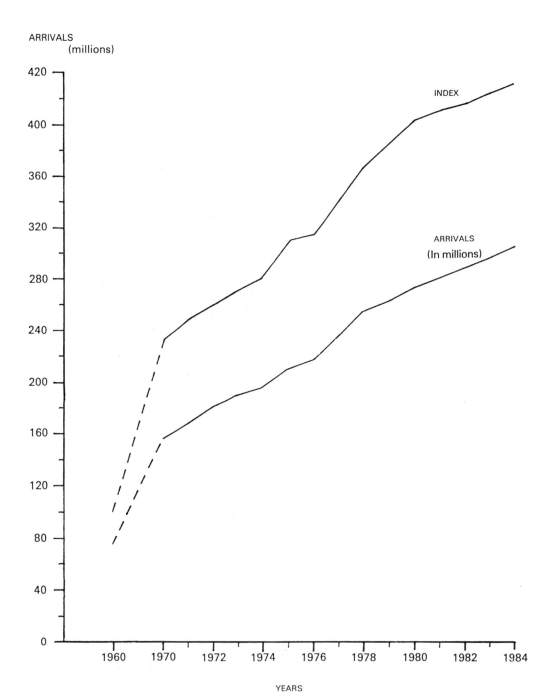

region also makes an indirect contribution to the economy, as receipts are re-spent within the country or region, thereby generating further income as the effects of the initial spending continue to filter through the economy. This issue is discussed in greater detail in Chapter 11 which considers the income 'multiplier effect' as this process is known.

Table 7
The Share of Tourist Activity in Total
Economic Activity, 1981

	Receipts as a % GDP			Expenditures as a % of PFC		
	Internal	Domestic	Total	Internal	Domestic	Total
Belgium & Luxembourg	1.6	1.7	3.3	4.2	2.7	6.9
Denmark	2.1	1.1	3.2	3.9	1.9	5.8
France	1.2	4.0	5.2	1.5	6.1	7.6
Germany	0.9	3.7	4.6	4.3	6.2	10.5
Greece	4.9	0.2	5.1	0.9	0.2	1.1
Ireland	3.1	0.8	3.9	5.2	1.3	6.5
Italy	2.1	1.8	3.9	0.7	2.8	3.5
Netherlands	1.2	2.1	3.3	4.7	3.7	8.4
UK	1.2	1.7	2.9	2.1	2.7	4.8
EUR-10	1.4	2.8	4.2	2.6	4.5	7.1

Sources: OECD, Tourism Policy and International Tourism, Paris, 1982, and Commission of the European Communities, European Economy, November 1981.

Factors Affecting the Development of International Tourism

The growth and development of international tourism can be influenced by direct government intervention in the management of tourist resources, especially in those countries where the tourist sector is an important element in the national development plan. However, the private sector usually has a crucial part to play in the development of tourist facilities.

The first stage is to develop an effective plan to market a locality for international tourists. In order to do this several basic questions must be asked, such as:

'What is the existing market for tourism from abroad?'
'What tourist products and services do we have?'
'What are the prospects for growth?'
'What will attract the potential visitors to the country?'
'What are the strengths and weaknesses of our tourist product?'
'What alternative destinations are there for international tourists?'
'Can our existing infrastructure cope with an increase in tourist numbers?'

In order to provide answers to these questions the public or private tourist organisation will have to carry out detailed research. This may be desk research or field research, and both of these methods are examined in more detail in Chapter 10.

At a material level development of international tourism can be encouraged by promoting a range of natural and created tourist facilities. For those countries with tourism potential where International tourism has not yet developed, the first task is to produce a detailed survey of existing tourist attractions whether they are natural (scenery, climate, wildlife), cultural (museums and galleries, theatres, historic buildings or sites) or entertainments. The process of planning and development of tourism is discussed in more detail in Chapter 9.

There are three general factors that will influence the development of international tourism, particularly in the developing regions of the world. These are:

(i)   a growth in lower cost long distance travel;

(ii)   provision of suitable accommodation and tourist facilities in the destination countries and a properly trained workforce to service them;

(iii)   a stable political and financial climate.

The introduction of larger aircraft such as the Boeing 747 has already had a dramatic impact on long-haul flights. The de-regulation of airline fares and the introduction of new types of aircraft with lower unit cost should enable lower fares to be introduced. The growth of inclusive tour packages should help to reduce the overall cost of international travel together with creative pricing policies for the off-peak season. Boeing forecasts, in its *Current Market Outlooks,* that annual increases in air travel in the 1990s will be greater than the total size of the market in 1960. One impetus to increased air travel will be the development of more fuel efficient engines and lighter airframes which will offer much greater operating range for aircraft. Improvements in aircraft technology will also enable aircraft to fly to long-haul destinations on two engines where three or four would have been necessary before.

During the 1990s the new generation Boeing 747 – 400 is expected to dominate the long-haul tourism market. Already non-stop flights are available to Hong Kong from the UK, and there will be an upward growth in non-stop flights between Europe and the Far East and the United States and Australasia. If the demand for international tourism continues as predicted, the Boeing company plan to launch a further aircraft, the 747 – 500 model, in the mid 1990s with a range of over 8,500 miles and over 500 seats.

The most dramatic growth in air travel is expected to be in Asia where its market share of world traffic is expected to increase from 25.8% in 1982 to 33.3% in 1992. (ICAO).

Having made it easier to travel from Europe to say the Seychelles or Sri Lanka it is important that the tourist destination has the infrastructure and trained staff to handle tourists en masse. Any new tourist facilities will be competing with much nearer and more familiar tourist attractions and will have to offer amenities and facilities that are of a high standard and at a competitive price. In breaking into a new market it is essential that the new tourist destination does not simply replicate facilities found all over Europe. The aim should be to develop distinctive facilities that relate to and enhance the atmosphere of the country

At the same time there is a need to develop and train a workforce for the newly-emerging tourist industry. The quality of service that international tourists receive is at least as important, if not more so, than the standard of tourist facilities. This training will need to take account of:

—   New techniques and technology, including computerised reservation and booking systems and modern production techniques particularly for food service and preparation.

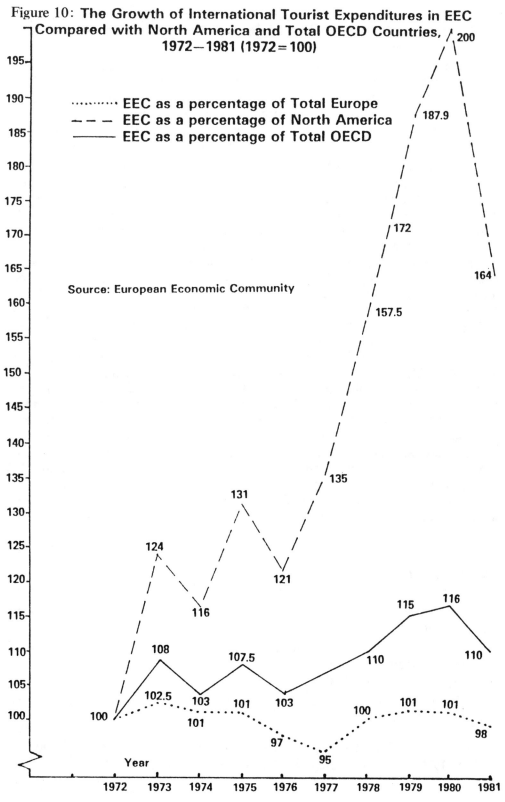

Figure 10: **The Growth of International Tourist Expenditures in EEC Compared with North America and Total OECD Countries, 1972–1981 (1972 = 100)**

Legend:
.... EEC as a percentage of Total Europe
– – – EEC as a percentage of North America
——— EEC as a percentage of Total OECD

Source: European Economic Community

- Restructuring employment in the tourism enterprise so as to increase the level of services. This is particularly important in developing countries where local unemployment levels may be high.
- Adapting training to improve the level and quality of personal service provided. Although more international tourists are opting for an informal, independent form of travel, the idea of personal service is becoming increasingly valued. Moreover, the search for greater cultural content in holidays and the development of special interest tourism provides increasing opportunities for careers in these tourist activities.

The importance of a stable political and financial climate is crucial for the future development of international tourism. Three quite different examples help to emphasise this point. In April 1986 President Reagan approved a bombing raid on Libya using aircraft based in Britain. One immediate repercussion was a dramatic decline in Americans travelling to Europe fearing terrorist reprisals. In Britain in May 1986 there were 40 per cent fewer Americans than in the same month in 1985. Overall in 1986 Britain lost about £300 million in tourist revenue because of the sharp fall in American tourists. The picture was worse on the Continent where US tourists were down 60 per cent in Greece and France and 50 per cent down in Italy. In Northern Ireland after 20 years of civil strife and bombings the international tourist industry, which once was thriving, has all but collapsed. In Sri Lanka, once a fast-growing tourist destination, the civil war has had similar impact on the tourist traffic, where the number of visitors between 1981 and 1984 fell by over 54,000. However, the current outlook is more promising.

A stable financial climate is important for two particular reasons. First the private sector needs to have confidence in the stability of the national economy before it will invest in tourism development projects, and often loans and other financial concessions will be necessary for the development of tourist facilities in the early stages. Secondly, exchange rates can play a major part in international travel, particularly to and from the United States. When the value of the US dollar is high compared to other (European) currencies this acts as a greater incentive for Americans to travel abroad. Conversely, a high value dollar will cause a sharp decline in the inflow of overseas visitors to the United States.

ASSIGNMENTS

1. Using data on international tourist arrivals for 1970 produce 2 maps to show the main tourist flows and identify:

   (a) the main tourist generating countries;
   (b) the main destinations;
   (c) the main links and routes between them.

   Give a brief account of the changes that have taken place in this period and suggest reasons for these.

2. Identify what you think will be the major international tourist destinations in the 1990s and justify the choices that you have made.

Chapter 5

The Retail Travel Sector

Learning Objectives: After reading this chapter you should have an introduction to the retail travel business and an understanding of:
— the range of services offered by the retail travel agent;
— the place of the retail travel sector in the tourist industry;
— the procedures involved in setting up and managing a travel agency;
— the relationship between travel agents and tour operators;
— job opportunities, total manpower needs, and the future of this sector of the tourist industry.

Introduction

The retail travel sector — in the form of the High Street travel agent — is the one activity most clearly recognised by the general public to represent the tourist industry. Travel agents have been in existence for over 100 years, with Thomas Cook pioneering the business. Although Thomas Cook began as a tour operator, the rapid growth in his business led to him opening an office in London and acting as a sales agent for several steamship lines and railway companies. By the end of the nineteenth century travel agencies had developed in the United States including American Express which as an offshoot of the Wells Fargo Company, borrowed Cook's idea of traveller's cheques in 1891.

However, it was not until the 1950s and 1960s that the number of travel agencies increased dramatically, this was due largely to two factors:

(i)   The large-scale growth of the commercial airlines. By the end of the 1930s there were over 50 commercial airlines worldwide flying over 200 million miles serving over 400,000 passengers. (Lickorish & Kershaw 1958). These commercial airlines soon discovered the benefits in allowing travel agents to promote their services and were willing to pay commissions for this.

(ii) The post-war growth in package tours beginning with the early charter flights and foreign holiday packages put together by enterprising tour operators who then used the retail travel agencies to sell this product. Now the bulk of the retail travel agents' business is package holidays.

In Britain there are now about 7,000 retail travel agents, 5,000 of whom are members of the Association of British Travel Agents (ABTA) and 2,000 who are non-members. In the United States there are about 30,000 retail travel agents.

Services Offered by the Travel Agent

Most tourists are unaware that the travel agent is acting on behalf of a third party. The travel agent is a retailer and with the exception of a few agents who are

43

also tour operators (for example Thomas Cook), the agent does not put together the tours or package holidays but only promotes or sells them on behalf of the tour operator. Most small towns and every city will have a number of travel agents in their main shopping district, and although there are a number of large national chains, many agencies are small in size, perhaps employing 4 or 5 staff.

What is the role and function of the travel agent?

The travel agent generally offers the following range of services:

— selling prepared package tours, preparing individual itineraries, personally escorted tours and group tours;
— arranging transport; selling airline tickets, rail, coach, and cruise trips and arranging car hire abroad;
— arranging hotels, motels, sightseeing trips, music festivals, transfers of passengers between terminals and hotels;
— handling and advising on many details involved in travel especially foreign travel such as travel and luggage insurance, medical insurance, travellers cheques, visa requirements and so on;
— providing information and advice on airline rail and coach schedules and fares; hotel rates; whether rooms have baths; whether their rates include local taxes. All of this information can take days of the intending tourists' time or weeks of endless phone calls and letters;
— arranging reservations for special interest activities such as business travel, sporting holidays, religious pilgrimages and so on;
— in the case of legitimate complaints from customers writing to the principal (tour operator or airline) to try and get a refund or a written statement or apology for any mishaps that may have occurred;
— interpreting and advising clients of the many complex discounted fares offered by the airlines and to warn clients of 'overbooking'.

The travel agency then represents all the package tour companies, all the airlines and all the coach and rail operators who use his services. A good travel agent will be able to advise the potential traveller on a wide range of matters concerning his journey, accommodation and final destination (holiday resort). The agent must therefore have a good knowledge of the product, and should know what he is selling. He is giving professional advice and if he has not been to an area or resort he is selling he can pick up information from trade journals, promotional material and current information from colleagues who know the area. In other words, the good agent should know where to go for current information on reliable tour operators and tourist destinations. Many small travel agencies may rely on tour operators brochures and thus offer a limited range of advice to their customers based on these brochures alone. However, there are a wide range of travel and accommodation directories available (mainly for Britain and the United States) and these provide a wealth of ancillary information on travel and accommodation which can be used to provide fast and accurate data.

Establishing a Travel Agency

The capital cost of setting up a retail travel agency is much less than for almost any other kind of retail business, because the agent requires relatively little in the form of stock. He is buying or leasing office space, viewdata systems with access to airlines and tour operators booking and information services, telephones and office equipment. The stock — in the form of brochures, tickets and related material, is supplied by the tour operator (wholesaler) or carrier (airline rail or coach company). In opening a travel agency the most critical step is finding the right location. This is related to several factors such as:

— identifying the market for your product and the type of clientele you wish to attract. The location must be in a neighbourhood that will service clients who will wish to take foreign package holidays, cruises, special interest holidays etc;

— the location of competitors. Although the Association of British Travel Agents does not object to new members on the grounds of a nearby competitor, the tour operators and transport operators may be less inclined to give agency agreements or licences;

— accessibility. Although much of the travel agent's business is conducted over the telephone or using telex or viewdata links, the agency must be visible and easily accessible to its customers. A ground-floor office in the main shopping and business district, with ample nearby parking is the ideal location;

— ample investment capital. Most airlines, for example will not give commission on the sale of tickets until the agency receives appointment as an official agent for the International Air Transport Association (IATA) and (in the United States) the Air Traffic Conference (ATC), and in Britain the domestic airlines and other transport operators. Approval or licences can take some time to obtain, and an agency should have at least 2 years operating capital available before it begins to make a profit from its operations.

Travel Agency Appointments and Commissions

The travel agency obtains the bulk of its income from commissions on the sale of its products, and to collect commissions must be officially appointed as an agent for the airline and transport companies and the tour operators (wholesalers). In the United States in order to be appointed as an official travel agent the firm must meet certain requirements set by 'conferences' representing the domestic and international airlines, shipping companies, railways and his companies. Each group has its own regulating board or 'conference'. The main conferences are the Air Traffic Conference (ATC) representing US domestic airlines, the International Air Transport Association (IATA); the international Passenger Ship Association (IPSA) and the Trans Pacific Conference (TPPC) which represents the Atlantic and Pacific shipping lines. Appointment by the Air Traffic Conference is the most important pre-requisite for a travel agency in the United States, and once obtained most of the other agency appointments are relatively straightforward. To obtain an ATC appointment the travel agency must be open for business; be operated under the direction of a qualified manager; have a good credit rating and (to protect the financial interests of the public and the airlines) have its operations investigated and approved by a bonding company who will guarantee responsibility for the agency's commitments up to $15,000 and sufficient funding to operate for one year without commission from the principal, and be actively involved in the production of travel.

In Britain to obtain commission on airline ticket sales a travel agency must obtain a licence from IATA. Since any retail agency obtains much of its income from commissions on the sale of airline tickets it is usually necessary to obtain an IATA appointment. IATA insists on similar requirements for retail travel agents as those sought by the Air Traffic Conference and in addition IATA requires that at least one employee have one year or more experience in international ticketing and reservations. Proof that the travel agency is actively promoting international air travel is also needed.

To obtain commission on package tour holidays offered by the main tour operators travel agents should be members of the Association of British Travel Agents (ABTA). Prospective members of ABTA must provide evidence of financial stability and deposit a bond (of £7,500 if they are a sole trader or £3,500 if a company) in favour of ABTA as financial protection to the Association. ABTA travel agents have the sole right to sell inclusive package tours of ABTA tour operators and they do not sell package tours arranged by non-ABTA companies. This is because ABTA has a retailer fund, paid for by members, which reimburses members of the public who have lost money following an ABTA member becoming bankrupt. This ABTA booking arrangement has been in existence since 1965 and is known in the trade as *Operation Stabiliser*.

In Britain there are about 2,000 non ABTA members, mainly located in London and the Home Counties. The most active and prominent of these are the 'bucket shops' offering discounts on regular and charter flights to the main holiday destinations. With the growth in air traffic in the 1970s and the increasing competition between the major carriers many of the airlines have established a practice in Britain of selling off unsold seats at large discounts through non-appointed travel agents. The spread and success of these 'bucket shops' is unwelcome competition for the IATA appointed travel agencies who, under the terms of their agreement, are not allowed to sell heavily discounted tickets. At the present time the ABTA/IATA agents are seeking agreement to be allowed to sell their tickets on the same basis.

Other travel services such as car hire companies, and hotels do not need individual agency appointments but will pay commissions for any reservations or bookings made by a travel agency that has been appointed as an official agent by the major travel and tourism organisations.

Commissions

Once the retail travel agent has been appointed to represent IATA, ATC or ABTA the agency immediately becomes eligible to receive commissions on the sale of any travel tickets or tour operators packages that are members of these associations. The amount of money the travel agency earns from these sales varies according to the supplier and the kind of service provided. (This issue is discussed in detail in the next section of this chapter). In general terms companies operating in the same sector of the tourist industry tend to offer the same rates of commission for specific similar services. The *rates* of commission tend to be set by the particular association. For example, IATA sets the rates for the international airline industry — at present this is generally about 8 to 10 per cent. In terms of domestic airline fares, de-regulation in Britain and the United States has meant that airlines are free to establish their own rates of commission, although most have kept to de-regulation levels. The Cruise lines at present pay 10 per cent commission and often pay higher commission for group bookings. Most tour operators generally pay 10 per cent commission and depending on the individual operator this percentage may increase with group booking or marked increase in sales during the year.

In Britain the limited restrictions on setting up as a retail travel agent led to a rapid increase in the number of High Street outlets during the 1960s and 1970s although the overall size of the market grew slowly in the 1970s. The pattern that emerged was that a large proportion of the volume of bookings was generated by a small proportion of highly productive retailers. In 1968 the Economist Intelligence Unit in a report on travel agency profitability (EIU 1968) found that 25 per cent of all agents were generating 78 per cent of all revenue and in 1971 90 per cent of bookings were produced by 100 agents.

One result of this pattern is that the brand leaders among the tour operators now concentrate their business on the more productive retail outlets. The most recent spur to improving efficiency and productivity among retailers is the introduction of credit card discount schemes for holidaymakers booking with Barclaycard and the TSB Trust Card (TTG January 1987).

A survey of travel agents remuneration carried out by Thornton Baker Associates on behalf of ABTA (1984), found that all the agents surveyed experienced a decline in profits between 1980 and 1983 (Thornton Baker 1984). However, those agents who concentrated on business travel showed the smallest decline, whilst the smaller agents who generally tend to be less profitable experienced the most severe decline in profits from 15% to 10%. It is clear that the larger agencies (i.e. with an income of over £500,000) are in a better position to introduce economies of scale in their operations than the smaller agents.

Sales of inclusive tours grew by 28% overall during this period although prices showed little change and commissions showed a marginal increase from 9.1% to 9.4%. Despite this growth in volume of sales, operating costs rose by over 30% in the same period, leading to the overall decline in profits. Two conclusions from this survey were that there was some scope for fundamental improvements in the efficiency of retail travel agents, and that the existing volume of business could be carried out through a smaller number of businesses.

Given that travel agents' income is largely made up of commissions paid by tour operators and other sources, calculated by reference to the value of business transacted, it is useful to look at the sources of turnover as a percentage of total turnover as an indicator of the average mix of business. These are set out in Table 8 below. The average mix of business changed very little, although inclusive tours increased in overall importance.

Table 8
Travel Agency Turnover as a Percentage of Total Rurnover 1980 – 83

Source	1980	1983
Inclusive Tours	% 52.3	% 54.5
Air Tickets	33.0	31.1
Rail Tickets	2.7	2.6
Ferry Tickets	2.4	2.3
Insurance	0.8	1.0
Car Hire	0.3	0.3
Other	8.5	8.2
Total	100.0	100.0

Source: Thornton-Baker ABTA Survey 1984

In the United States airline de-regulation and the growth in the usage of computer reservation systems have had a considerable impact on retail travel agents over the past 10 years. Although there are now about 30,000 travel agents in the USA, just 7% of them account for 28% of agency sales, and the picture has been one of fewer agents doing more business. In many cases declining profits have led to amalgamation and many agents have formed or joined chains that are able to offer good national coverage and the kinds of discounts on air tickets, hotel rooms and car rentals that come with volume of business.

Business Travel

The business travel sector is often the most profitable element of retail travel and it is a fast-growing sector of the travel market, as Figure 11 clearly shows. The UK market for all business travel is now worth over £17 billion a year, and the volume and spending on this sector has more than doubled since 1978. The travel and tourism industry has responded to the growth in this sector of the market by providing special incentives for business travellers, with hotels, airlines and car rental companies stressing first class service and competitive price packages.

Figure 11: Spending on business travel 1978-86

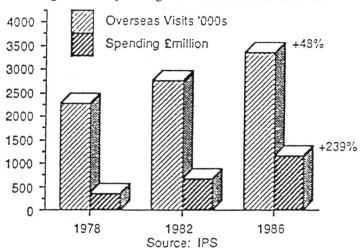

Source: IPS

In the United States business travel is now the third largest area of corporate expenditure, after salaries and data processing. (ABC International 1988). The worldwide boom in business and the growth of conference and exhibition centres have all contributed to the expansion in this sector. Globally business travel is estimated to be in excess of $150 billion. A recent study of over 17,500 passengers on international scheduled airline flights found that 85% of them were flying on business.

The larger well established multiple retail travel chains are the market leaders in UK Business travel. For example, Thomas Cook has 6,000 business clients managed through about 80 specialist travel centres. Hogg Robinson travel handles more than £175 million worth of business each year for 1,700 companies. In the United

States Hogg Robinson is a member of Woodside Management Systems which is one of the largest consortia of travel agents in the US market. Pickfords Business Travel (which recently took over Lunn Poly's Business Travel) is the third largest company dealing in this sector.

One measure of the growth in the market segment has been the growing interest in it by the financial services sector, with firms from American Express to Access and Visa and many others offering a wide range of travel support products from accessories and valet service to worldwide insurance and money supply.

If retail travel agents are to capture a share of this important market they need to be able to offer an efficient and cost effective service for the corporate client. This involves five main stages in business travel planning:

1. Setting out the guidelines by which executives travel and the ways in which travel arrangements are made.

2. Seeking out the most effective and value for money travel arrangements and those hotels or car rental companies that offer the best corporate rates.

3. The trip itself. It is important to be able to change the travel itinerary at short notice and to have an efficient system for settling expenses.

4. There is a need to guarantee corporate clients that company money is being used efficiently and properly, that corporate travel policy is followed and that the system is easy to administer. An effective travel expense system must be able to list specific costs incurred, explain the reasons for these and identify hidden costs that might go unnoticed. Expense reporting, payment, overdue claims and reconciliation are all included here.

5. Finally there is the review and analysis phase of corporate travel, which provides the opportunity to review existing company procedures and the development of more cost effective systems both for the retail travel agent and the company who are the client.

The growing use of personal computers in High Street travel agents will make this whole process more feasible by enabling them to establish databases on business travel and to improve their existing accounting and administration. In Chapter 13 this is discussed in more detail in the section dealing with the application of information technology to the travel and tourism industry.

Travel Agency Operations

It is clear from the evidence above that only a limited number of retail travel agents are highly profitable. The lesson is that although in Britain it is relatively easy to set up in business as a retail travel agent it is much more difficult to achieve a worthwhile level of profitability even after 2 years of trading.

The Economist Intelligence Unit's *Survey of the British Travel Industry* (EIU 1968) found that most travel agencies kept inadequate financial information on revenue and expenditure, generally because the accounts were prepared, not for the agency manager, but for the major carriers and the Inland Revenue. There is a need therefore to establish a system of financial planning which provides a cash flow analysis/projection of the agencies' actual and estimated income and ex-

Figure 12: Links in the Retail Travel Sector

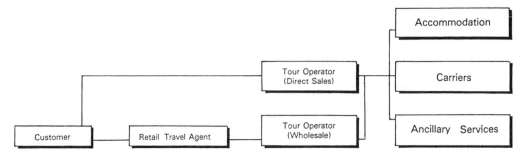

penses on a weekly, monthly, seasonal and annual basis. With this kind of information the agency owner/manager can identify how the business is performing or likely to perform and can identify weaknesses in the operation and goals to be achieved in terms of improved sales performance, new target markets and so on.

Given that the travel agent is offering a *service* and *selling* a product it is *time* that is the most valuable component in his operation. An analysis of sales performance over the year can help identify the 'quiet' periods in the operation of the business when files can be updated, mailing lists reviewed, familiarisation visits organised and business plans for the coming year updated. Having done this he needs also to analyse the operation of the office and the book-keeping and reservations systems.

Booking an airline ticket may take 20 minutes or several hours depending on the knowledge of the client and the experience of the travel agency staff. Access to computerised information and centralised booking systems can greatly speed up this process.

When small travel agents are declared bankrupt (and 55 went bankrupt in 1985) (ABTA 1986), three contributing factors generally exist:

(i)   poor financial planning, due to inadequate records or failure to use available financial information;

(ii) poor market analysis and management of sales;

(iii) failure to offset general administration costs by additional revenues.

Good financial control can help identify where things are going wrong or going well in the business. There is a need therefore to produce a budget showing expenditure and income from commissions on a regular basis and link this to an accounting system which shows deviations from the planned budget. If the budget does not balance there are two possible courses of action; increase sales without increasing the overhead; or increase income by reducing the overhead. This process can be helped by analysing the nature of the firm's business over the past year and dropping those areas or clients that are not providing value for money.

Tour Operators

Tour operators plan, price, package and market an inclusive foreign holiday. They are the 'manufacturing' element of the tourist industry. Most tour operators are wholesalers in that they produce a package holiday and negotiate with retail travel agents who then sell this product. Some tour operators such as Thomas Cook and American Express are both wholesalers and retailers.

There are three types of tour operator:

1. *Direct sell* tour operators who by-pass the High Street travel agent and sell directly to the public. They will put together package holidays and advertise and sell to their own clientele. The operator may be a small agency or a multi-branch organisation that markets thousands of tours.

2. *Wholesale* operators who do not deal directly with the public and who put together and operate tours exclusively through travel agents. They do not accept direct bookings and have no direct contact with the public.

3. *General Tour Contractors* These are tour operators who do not package and promote their own tours. Instead reservations are forwarded to local contractors or to wholesalers. Organisations such as British Airways who brought the direct-sell operator Martin Rooks, or special affinity groups organising travel to North America or Australasia, or non-profit organisations all come into this category.

Organising Tour Operations

The Tour Operator must be planning the inclusive holiday package at least one to two years before the first departure date and tours for some events such as the World Cup or the Olympics or the Passion Play at Oberammergau have to be planned years in advance. The first 5 to 6 months will be spent in putting a saleable package together, that is chartering aircraft, arranging transfers to coaches or ferries, booking hotel rooms, meals and arranging sightseeing tours. The next 4 to 5 months will be spent laying out and printing promotional material. The tour operator then spends 4 to 6 months checking up on new places and tourist developments and hotel operations. Tour testing is an important element in designing package tours and most operators will sample more than once before the package is made available to the public, to iron out any snags in the tour arrangements.

The three main elements of a tour package are the cost of the transport, the hotel accommodation and the ancillary services. Some companies have *integrated operations* where the tour operator has acquired or established its own airline. For example Horizon Holidays has established Orion Airways, Intasun (part of the International Leisure Group) has developed Air Europe, Martin Rooks, whose parent company is British Airways, uses the British Airways subsidiary British Air Tours, and the International Thomson Organisation own Britannia Airways.

Mass Market Tour Operations

One of the most competitive parts of the holiday package tour business is inclusive air tours. The market is now dominated by three main operators International Thomson Organisation, International Leisure Group and Horizon Holidays. These three companies supplied 37 per cent of the market in 1981. In 1987 they accounted for 70 per cent of the market. The economies of scale available to the larger operators gives them such a cost advantage that it becomes harder and harder for the smaller companies to compete unless they specialise,

Figure 13: Growth of Inclusive Air Tours 1981 – 1987

Carving up the holiday market
Estimated Market Share

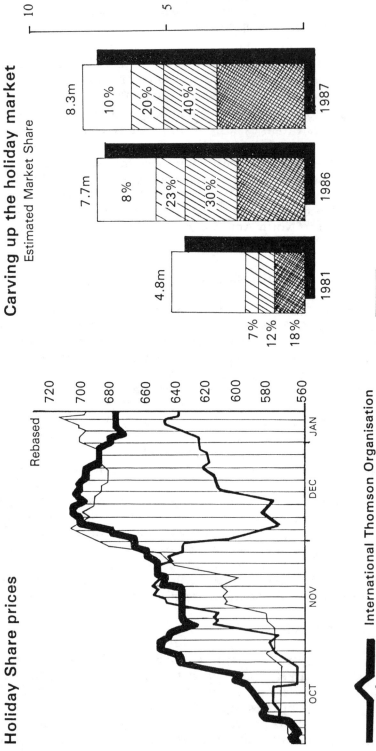

8.3m 10% 20% 40%

7.7m 8% 23% 30%

4.8m 7% 12% 18%

1987 1986 1981

Horizon Travel

International Leisure Group

International Thomson Organisation

Holiday Share prices

Rebased
720
700
680
660
640
620
600
580
560

OCT   NOV   DEC   JAN

International Thomson Organisation

International Leisure Group

Horizon Travel

Source: *The Times* 12.1.87

and the high cost of entry into the business means that a competitor once squeezed out is less likely to be replaced.

The hotel accommodation forms the second main part of the holiday package and here the tour operator buys bed space or guarantees a specific number of rooms to the hotel management. By 'guaranteeing' rooms he must pay for them whether they are sold or not. Location of the property is another prime factor as is the grade and type of hotel. Problems occur from time to time when hotels oversell their bedspace in the expectation that some bookings will be cancelled, and then are unable to cope with the influx of tourists who expect accommodation. Negotiations with National Tourist Associations and Trade Associations are helping to overcome this problem.

With the growth of UK consumer spending on foreign holidays during the 1980s the competition for the mass market has been fierce. In 1981 4.8 million people took package tours abroad and of these the Thomson Group had 18 per cent of the market, the International Leisure Group (Intasun) had 12 per cent, and Horizon 7 per cent. The remaining 63 per cent was handled by a number of smaller firms. By 1988 inclusive air tours had trebled in volume to 14.5 million (Civil Aviation Authority). The market share is dominated by four companies who between them have 62% of the total holidays business. These are the Thompson Group, the International Leisure Group, Redwing Holidays and the Owners Abroad Group. Redwing increased their market share dramatically in 1987/8 when they acquired British Airways Holidays Ltd following its sale by the parent company British Airways. The growth of these four companies underlines the importance of size to profitability in the tour operations business. Many of the normal risks can then be reduced or removed. Forward buying can provide a hedge against currency changes and companies can impose fuel surcharges of up to £10 if fuel prices increase.

High volumes of business also reduce overheads per holiday and increase an operators ability to buy aircraft seats or hotel beds at competitive prices. In all of this it is the smaller tour operators who will be squeezed out as they lose their market share and competitive edge in bidding for hotel bedspaces and aircraft seats.

Tour operations can be a high risk business and often profit margins are very slim. For example despite an increase of 31% in turnover in 1987 over 1986 from £2.1 billion to £2,8 billion 11 of the top 30 tour operators made losses of £48.3 million while the remaining 19 companies made profits of £23.5 million (Civil Aviation Authority 1988). These disappointing returns reflected the very fierce competition among tour operators and in 1987 many holidays were sold at prices which were just not viable. Tour operators need to strike a balance between volume and profitability.

In the UK the twenty largest tour operators established a voluntary association known as the Tour Operators Study Group (TOSG) which provides a forum for its members to meet and discuss matters of common interest and as a major negotiating body with foreign Hotel Associations and Governments/National Tourist Associations.

Employment in the Retail Travel Trade

The growth in High Street travel agents during the 1970s led to a growth in a wide range of clerical and administrative jobs in both travel agencies and tour operators (English Tourist Board/Institute of Manpower Studies in 1986). Counter and reservations staff account for about 14,000 employees with a further 2,500 managers and related staff. About three-quarters of these people work in the High Street travel agencies and about two-thirds of counter and reservations staff are women. The age profile of agency staff is quite young with most staff in their 20s and promotion prospects for suitably qualified and experienced staff have been good.

In addition, most, if not all, tour operators employ tour escorts or representatives who are key elements in a successful tour operation. These are professionals who should be fluent in the local language, have an extensive knowledge of the area, and sufficient experience to deal with the logistics of transferring tourists and the luggage to their hotels, dealing with a myriad number of complaints and having a good public relations sense. British Companies probably employ about 2,000 carriers and resort representatives overseas, mostly on six to seven month fixed-term contracts.

ASSIGNMENTS

1. Using your local copy of *Yellow Pages* identify the location and type of travel agencies listed. Selecting, say 10 in one large town, identify their location and plot this on a street plan. What locational characteristics do they show? How many are:

    (a) General travel agents?
    (b) Specialised travel agents?
    (c) Branches of larger chains?
    (d) Independent retailers?
    (e) Members of ABTA/IATA?

2. You are the manager of a small retail travel agency located in the main central shopping area. Next door is a camera shop, and across the road is a bank and a sports shop. Design a joint advertising campaign that will link all of these businesses to the travel agency and increase your turnover in package tour sales.

Chapter 6

The Passenger Transport Sector

Learning Objectives: After reading this chapter you should understand:

— the importance to the tourist industry of air, sea, rail and road transport
— the effects of regulation and de-regulation of transport
— the impact on tourist resorts/tourist regions following the growth in car ownership since the 1950s
— the role of public and private transport in Britain
— the levels of tourism-related employment in the passenger transport sector.

Introduction

As Chapter 2 and Chapter 4 demonstrate, the growth of mass tourism is closely linked with improvements in the means of transport. These improvements enabled the main carriers to transport people in much greater numbers than before, and to lower the unit cost of this travel, making the opportunity to travel available to a much greater proportion of the public. In addition, the speed of travel has increased considerably over the past 30 years so that trains travelling at 125 miles an hour and passenger aircraft at 500 miles an hour are commonplace. This has had the effect of shortening journey times and of bringing more distant destinations within the reach of the average traveller. Journey time and also reduced unit cost, due to greater utilisation of vehicles and accessibility are key factors to be considered when a tour operator puts an inclusive tour together, and the inclusion in mass market brochures of regions such as the Gambia or the Seychelles is a result of reducing journey times from Europe to these more distant destinations. It has also meant that more countries have to cope with the impact of mass tourism on the environment, and the issues that this raises are discussed in detail in Chapter 12.

Road transport was largely horse-drawn and still slow and subject to frequent stops to rest the horses, and it was the growth of rail and sea transport during the second half of the nineteenth century that had a significant influence on the types of tourism and tourist resort that developed. The rail and sea routes were developed to transport freight, but their presence and their shorter journey times attracted passengers especially in the hinterland of the major cities where the railways provided a quick and reliable means of journey to work.

Rail Transport

Chapter 2 described the growth of seaside resorts in Victorian England following the invention of the railway and the development of rail links between the

Table 9

Mode of Travel to Holiday 1951—81

Year	Car	Rail	Bus or Coach
1951	28%	48%	24%
1961	49%	28%	23%
1971	63%	10%	17%
1981	72%	12%	12%

Source: ETB Annual Reports

resorts and the main centres of population. By the end of the nineteenth century most tourists arrived by rail and the land use pattern of the resort reflects their development during the railway age, even though today rail travel is much less important for mass tourism.

Rail travel in Britain was organised on a regional basis until the railways were nationalised to form British Rail in 1947. If we concentrate on their passenger carrying role, BR divide their railway business into three sectors:

(i)   Inter-City

(ii)   London and the South East

(iii)   Provincial services

The inter-city network covers six main routes (Fig 14 on page 58) radiating outward from London, and it is this network and the provincial services that are mainly used by tourists. The London and South East network is mainly commuter traffic although it does handle day trippers to Brighton, Southend and the North Kent resorts.

Although the railways monopolised the mass travel market during the nineteenth century they suffered from competition from coach and car transport during the twentieth century and more recently lost traffic to the airlines, particularly in the United States. This was in part due to their failure to recognise the importance of the mass travel market, possibly conditioned by the priority given to the freight and parcels services. The increasing competition from road freight operations and a decline in revenue during the 1950s led to a drastic overhaul of British Rail's operations in the early 1960s. The Beeching Report *The Reshaping of British Railways* led to a drastic reduction in the overall size and geographic extent of the rail network, particularly serving rural areas many of which are tourist destinations.

It was not until the 1970s that British Rail began to review its marketing policies for passenger transport, and to some extent this was due to the threat to its monopoly on internal long-distance travel in the UK from the private car, coach and airline companies who had become much more competitive. BR established a Golden Rail subsidiary in 1972 based in York. This organisation began to market 'Golden Rail' holidays where BR offered an all-in package including travel and accommodation. The accommodation was provided by BR and the major hotel chains. As the market developed destinations such as Amsterdam and Paris were included in the brochures. These tours were sold either through the main BR sta-

Growth of BR Golden Rail Short Stay Holidays 1980—86

YEAR	TYPE OF HOLIDAY				
	Short Stay		Long Stay		Total
	000s	%	000s	%	000s
1980	78	(17)	138	(83)	166
1981	29	(21)	108	(79)	137
1982	35	(31)	78	(69)	113
1983	71	(52)	65	(48)	136
1984	109	(67)	54	(33)	163
1985	130	(77)	39	(23)	169
1986	135	(78)	39	(22)	174

Source: Report of Transport and Tourism Conference 1986 OTTS

tions or high street travel agents. The success of the 'Golden Rail' concept can be seen from Table 10 which shows that the volume of traffic increased to 174,000 in 1986. Encouraged by this tactic British rail began to market short break and 'mini-holiday' packages, with special discounts for out of season breaks, using rail travel to major tourist resorts and with tie ins to the main hotels there. As they have a large control over the *rail* market BR realised that they had much more opportunity to use price discrimination and to target their efforts on particular segments of the market who could be attracted to the benefits of special travel offers. Their development of senior citizens railcards and student railcards is part of this policy.

Private Railway Lines

There has been a resurgence of interest in private railway lines as many local preservation societies and steam rail enthusiasts have rescued local branch lines after their closure by BR. Some of these are standard gauge lines such as the Nene Valley Railway (near Peterborough), the Watercress Line (in Hampshire), the Bluebell Line (in Sussex) or the Severn Valley Railway. Others are narrow gauge lines such as the Romney, Hythe and Dymchurch railway in Kent, the Ravenglass and Eskdale line in Cumbria, or the 'Great Little Trains of Wales'. They are all now mainly tourist attractions relying on income from tourists during the season, donations from the public and the unpaid services of enthusiasts.

Road Transport: (1)   The Private Car

The growth in private car ownership with most families either arriving or having access to at least one car, is a relatively recent phenomenon. But it has had a dramatic impact on the types of holiday that people take as well as on the environment of the resorts and holiday regions. Table 9 on page 56 highlights the growth

Figure 14: The Main BR Inter-City Rail Network

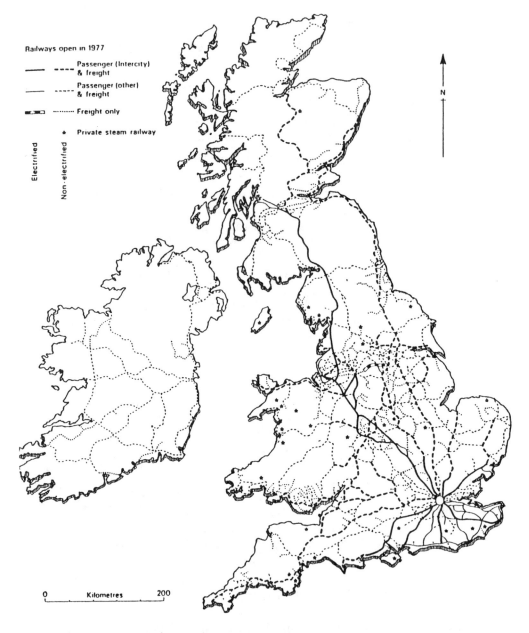

The present railway network.

in car useage between 1951 and 1986. In 1951 only 27 per cent of holidaymakers travelled by car to the main UK holiday destinations. In 1986 over two-thirds travelled by car. In 1960 there were 5.7 million private cars in Britain. Today there are 16 million. As the number of car owning households increases, and as more households acquire a second car, the private car will continue to dominate the domestic tourist scene in Britain, the United States and most European countries. In the peak summer period a considerable proportion of the road traffic travelling to the south of France or through Germany and Switzerland to Italy, is generated by tourists in private cars.

Assuming a reasonable road system, the private car provides an unrivalled degree of mobility for the tourist and it provides a degree of convenience not offered by any other form of transport. It enables the tourist to travel from his home to his destination with all his family and luggage with the minimum amount of transfer and without having a rigid timetable. Once at the tourist resort the car enables the tourist to gain access to the surrounding tourist region.

In addition, use of the private car for holiday travel is perceived by the tourist as being cheaper than other modes of travel. Although it is expensive to acquire a car, once bought the cost of journeys is relatively small, particularly if several passengers are carried, and most drivers just calculate the cost of oil and petrol when considering using the car for holiday travel.

The growth in car ownership has also led to a growing preference for touring holidays where resorts are now seen as a base from which to visit a much wider hinterland. Resorts have to face competition from a wide range of attractions in the surrounding region, and indeed many now market these attractions as part of the overall 'appeal' of the resort.

In Britain and Europe there has been a corresponding growth in the ownership of touring caravans and campers and this trend has affected the tourist resorts and holiday regions in two ways. First, the traditional forms of holiday accommodation have lost some of their market share as caravanning and camping has increased. Secondly, the proliferation of caravans and tents has spread from the fringes of the traditional seaside resort into the formerly less accessible parts of the tourist regions creating significant planning problems. This issue is discussed in more detail in Chapter 12.

In the United States there has been corresponding growth in recreational vehicles (RVs), from 80,300 in 1962 to over 7.5 million in 1986. The growth of camping in the United States has encouraged the creation of a nationwide consortium of campgrounds (Camp Coast to Coast) representing over 400 campground owners. Most of the users of these campgrounds arrive in recreational vehicles. One in ten Americans own a recreational vehicle. (*USA Today* 1986).

Road Transport: (2) Coach Transport

Most resort towns will have a variety of outlets selling coach excursions to the surrounding area, particular beauty spots or evening concerts. Nearly 90% of the excursions and tours business is run by private operators, and this proportion will increase as de-regulation of the coach business comes into effect. Most of these firms are small in size, often having less then 6 vehicles (Transport Statistics HMSO 1981).

Coach travel was at its heyday in the 1920s and 1930s and as early as 1920

British coaches ran six-day tours of the battlefields of France and Flanders (Taylor 1956). By 1939 37 million passengers were carried on regular long distance services and tours, and of these over 10,000 were taken on continental tours by British coaches. By 1955 there were 100 million passenger journeys on long distance services and tours (Lickorish 1958). However, the growth in car ownership since the 1950s has led to a gradual decline in the numbers travelling by coach, although it is still a significant element of passenger transport and has increased again since 1980.

Coach transport has several functions. It can provide:

a)   Express services between major cities and major tourist resorts;
b)   Group travel for special interest groups, associations and so on;
c)   Transfers between airport or ferry terminals and hotels;
d)   Tours and Excursions.

The advantage of coach travel is that like the private car it is very flexible and accessible, particularly in rural areas, and is relatively cheap. The unit cost of a full coach is less than that of the individual private car. This economy is passed on to the passenger and coach fares generally undercut rail fares for journeys between the same towns. The much lower cost of long-distance coach travel has attracted a growing share of the younger tourist market and has encouraged some firms to develop routes through Europe as far as Greece. Some tour operators now offer a 2 week coach and camping holiday in the south of France for under £250 at the height of the season — taking advantage of low travel and low accommodation costs.

Tours and excursions come under two categories. The first are local, based on individual resorts and providing a variety of day and half day excursions to tourist attractions in the surrounding hinterland. The second type are long-distance tours, for example through Scotland or parts of Europe, usually of 8 to 14 days duration. These are packaged to include couriers, overnight stops and local tours from the main resorts on the itinerary. These tours appeal to the elderly and retired in that they offer a local pick-up service, a courier to deal with any day-to-day problems and language difficulties, and the transport of heavy luggage right to the hotel. Often a spirit of 'camaraderie' builds up between the coach passengers, driver and courier, and the companies in this field find that they have a high level of repeat business.

The de-regulation of the coach transport business was from October 1980 following the 1980 *Transport Act*. This ended the licensing regulations affecting express coach routes and tours and excursions of over 30 miles. This led to a short-lived price war on several express routes between a consortium of private coach companies (British Coachways) and the publicly owned National Bus Company. Up to 1986 the market was still dominated by the National Bus Company which was administered through a network of 70 regional groups employing over 70,000 people with a fleet of 17,000 vehicles. One important effect of the 1980 Act was that the coach companies with more competitive fares and improved quality of vehicles with videos, toilets etc., won a greater share of the travel market mainly at the expense of British Rail.

The 1985 Transport Act had as one of its main objectives privatising the National Bus Company and by wholesale de-regulation to open up the market to private operators on any route. A programme is now under way to sell off the 70 regional groups and many may be subject to management buy-outs.

The 1980 de-regulation of express services is generally thought to have produced faster, cheaper and more luxurious coaches and it was these results among other experiments that prompted the move to complete de-regulation in 1985. The coach travel related to tourism will tend to gain from competition especially on the main routes between the major towns and cities and the irregular services such as excursions or transfers. The larger independent operators will continue to dominate the express and touring market, but there will be more scope for the smaller firms with their lower overheads to compete for excursion traffic and feeder routes. It is almost certain that while de-regulation will make coach operations more competitive, some of the independent operators will go bankrupt — particularly those who are least experienced in this business. Coach companies wishing to develop their tourist trade will increasingly rely on entrepreneurial senior managers to develop and maintain their market share.

In the United States President Reagan signed a Bill in 1982 which deregulated the coach industry, opening it for competition. Since then about 1,700 new bus companies have received Interstate Commerce Commission operating authority and there are now 3,500 operating bus companies in the United States (US Travel Data Centre 1985). Many of these new companies, just like their counterparts in Britain, are small but aggressive. The result is that a number of the old established bus companies perhaps 45 to 50 have gone out of business faced with a strong downward pressure on prices for charters and tours. The average fare paid by a charter or tour passenger dropped from $10.57 in 1982 to $8.80 in 1984. Although fares went down, ridership went up, and there was an increase of 4 million passengers on charters and tours in 1984 (US Travel Data Centre).

However, since de-regulation, profitability has declined steadily in the face of cuts in fares and as in Britain, this will affect the larger carriers more since they have a higher cost structure with higher overheads.

Maritime Transport

This can be divided into three categories, two of which are strictly maritime:

    (i)   Cruises and ocean-going ships
    (ii)   Ferries
    (iii)   Services on Lakes, inland waters and canals.

The main shipping lines who organise cruises or ocean-going passenger routes have established two conferences to represent their interests in the tourist industry. These are the International Passenger Ship Associates (IPSA) and the Trans Pacific Passenger Conference (TPPC) which represent the Pacific and Atlantic shipping companies.

Cruise Ships

Until the 1930s steamships provided the only means of long distance transport between the major continents and the growth of air travel, especially of inclusive air tours has had a severe impact on the shipping lines. In the post-war years they were faced with increasing competition from the airlines, rising operating costs and growing obsolescence in their shipping fleets and very high rebuilding/refitting costs. Most companies chose to diversify into other areas of activity and now those that remain have turned increasingly to the cruise line business. This is the luxury end of the tourist market. For example, only 4% of the population of the United States has taken a cruise, but the majority of that 4% is repeat business. The tourists on a cruise ship are not just buying a trip from A to B, they are buying a stay at a floating resort, with a level of service and accommodation comparable to the best resorts and hotels. The appeal of the cruise is that it is an all-inclusive package, with accommodation, meals and entertainment all included in the price of a ticket.

In the past 10 years the cruise lines have introduced innovations and special interest packages to appeal to a wider clientele. Most cruise lines offer a fly-cruise deal for example where passengers fly out to the Caribbean before joining the cruise ship in the West Indies. The most prestigious is probably the Cunard package which involves flying out of Britain to the United States on Concorde and returning on the QE2. The appeal to passengers of these fly-cruise packages is that in the past when cruises started at Southampton or New York, it took several days of sailing through cold waters and possibly rough seas before warmer waters were reached. Now tropical sunshine and warm waters are just several hours travel away.

In order to appeal to a younger clientele many cruise ships now offer full spa and fitness facilities as well as a wide range of sporting activities. For example, the Norwegian Caribbean Lines offer snorkeling and scuba diving lessons on board by qualified instructors; golf and tennis clinics are available on many ships. Some companies offer unique cruises for example, the Sun Line have an Amazon River Cruise that includes a performance at the Opera House Manaus and their Trans atlantic Grand Cruise begins in Athens and ends in Fort Lauderdale, with stops in the eastern and western Mediterranean and the Caribbean. The three main centres for cruise trips are the Caribbean, the Mediterranean and the Far East. The cruise market is dominated by United States tourists, who account for 80% of all cruise passengers, although the headquarters of the main cruise line companies are based in Europe. For Caribbean sailings many lines now fly passengers to San Juan, Puerto Rico or Jamaica or Barbados, or cruises begin at the Florida Ports. The west coast cities of Los Angeles, San Francisco and San Diego are attracting more cruise lines and are beginning to rival the Florida based lines, especially for Mexico and Panama Canal cruises.

In the Pacific more cruise lines are offering seven day cruises from Hong Kong and the ships of the Holland America, Cunard, Royal Viking and P&O Lines offer larger cruises calling in at Hawaii, Tahiti, New Zealand, Australia and Japan.

In Europe, DFDS Danish Seaways took over for Line and the West German Prinsferries in the early 1980s and built up a separate inclusive tour operation of short cruises outbound from UK ports to Scandinavia. These now account for 100,000 passengers a year out of a total of 1.2 million carried. About 30,000 of these are from the USA (Travel and Tourism Analyst 1987) and 45,000 from the UK.

Cruise ships are very labour intensive and average about one crew member for every two passengers. In other words a ship carrying 800 passengers should have about 400 crew members. Cruise ships vary in size from the relatively small ship carrying 100 passengers to the luxury liner carrying 900 to 1000 passengers, with cinemas, swimming pools and a wide range of onboard entertainment facilities.

The best data source is the *OAG Worldwide Cruise and Shipline Guide* which is published every two months. This provides information on shipping companies, ship profiles of individual ships, port terminal diagrams, cruise listings and itineraries and a wide range of ancillary information.

Passenger Ferries

The first steam passage of the Channel was in 1816 and the first regular steamer service in 1820. By the 1830s about 100,000 passengers were using the cross-Channel Ferries and by 1882 this had increased to 500,000. The present-day cross channel traffic carries 2.3 million passengers a year between seven different English ports and France, and on the east coast three ports operate ferry services across the North Sea (Fig 15 on page 64)

In the United States with the exception of the Mississippi river cruise lines, and the Great Lakes cruise ships there has not been a similar massive development in ferries linking different parts of the country. The American seamen's unions and restrictions by intracoastal transportation laws which prohibit traffic between USA ports, have prevented any development of shipping links.

The other main concentration of ferry routes is in the Mediterranean, particularly the links between mainland Spain, France, Italy and Greece and the islands that form part of their jurisdiction, where there is an extensive network of ferry links. Greece is a good example. There are over 20 main islands in the Aegean and Ionean seas and dozens of smaller ones and all of them rely on ferry services to bring in supplies and essential goods and of course, tourists. The ferry may be a car ferry of several thousand tons or an ultra modern hydrofoil providing a link between an airport and surrounding islands.

There are several key factors that determine the viability of ferry services:
(i)   They need to be equipped to deal with large numbers of passengers and their cars;
(ii)   they need to be equipped for a fast turn-round at their destination port at either end of the ferry link so as to increase the number of sailings during the peak season;
(iii) they require a roughly equal flow of traffic in both directions so that they have no 'dead' journeys;
(iv)   they need to be on routes that provide a good year-round flow of traffic.

The cross channel routes are all operated by roll on/roll off ferry services which minimise the time spent in port and provide a fast efficient service for car travellers. Over 3 million Britons take cars abroad each year and the only threat to the cross channel ferry services is the advent of the Channel Tunnel. In addition to the conventional ferry services, jet foil, hydrofoil, and hovercraft services offer high-speed water-borne links between Britain and the Continent.

Great improvements in the efficiency of ferry operations have occurred over the past 25 years. In 1953 it took up to 2½ hours for a small drive-on drive-off ship with a stern door to unload and re-load in port. By 1962 a drive through ship with

Figure 15: Sealink route map

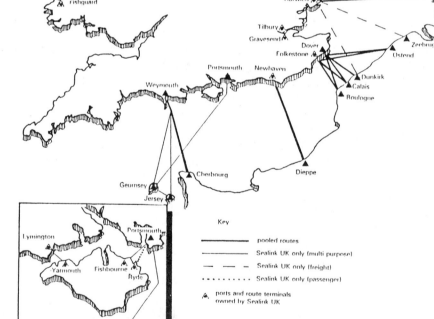

120 cars and 180 passengers took 1½ hours. Today a ferry taking 350 cars and 1,350 passengers can be turned round in 1 hour.

The English Channel and North Sea crossings from the UK to the continent carried an estimated 23 million passengers in 1985. Most of these were car-based holidaymakers. In the late 1950s there were just four car ferries operating. There are now over 200 ferry services around North West Europe, most of them serving the UK. In the 1970s there was a steady growth in passenger traffic through UK ports and the number of passengers almost doubled between 1975 and 1985 (Table 11). The Channel ferries, which account for about 75% of total crossings from the UK, are dominated by two companies, Sealink and P and O European ferries (formerly Townsend Thoresen). In recent years both companies have been engaged in fierce competition to protect and increase their market share in the face of the forthcoming threat of the channel tunnel.

Table 11:
Growth of Channel/North Sea Ferry Traffic 1975 – 1985

Year	1975	1976	1977	1978	1979	1980	1981	1982	1983	1984	1985
Passengers (millions)	13.89	14.78	16.09	17.4	18.73	20.89	22.6	23.62	23.86	23.17	23.24

Impact of the Channel Tunnel

The approval of the project to build a Channel Tunnel, scheduled for completion in 1993, will have a significant impact on ferry traffic. This is at a time when several ports, in particular Dover, have invested many millions of pounds in development programmes. Eurotunnel are forecasting a London to Paris journey time of 3 hours 15 minutes compared to 6 hours 45 minutes for a ferry crossing. This reduction in travel time, together with a probable very competitive price, will pose the most serious threat ever to the viability of these ferry services. Although Eurotunnel expect to create new markets as a result of the new fixed link, it is difficult to estimate how much of the traffic generated will be captured from existing ferry or airline routes.

Air Transport

This has been the most rapidly expanding Transport sector over the past 30 years and is now the main form of long distance travel. The great increase in inclusive package tours abroad has been largely due to advances in aircraft design and performance, with the long-haul market now dominated by wide-bodied jets carrying over 500 passengers at speeds averaging 600 mph for several thousand miles, and smaller capacity jets for the short-haul routes.

Between 1974 and 1984 the number of airline passengers carried world-wide increased by 66%, with the main increase occuring between 1974 and 1979 (Fig. 16 on page 67). During the same period the number of passenger/kilometres almost doubled (Table 12 on page 66). The market share was redistributed over this period with a decline in the North American and European share and a rapid increase in the airlines of East Asia and the Pacific (Table 13 on page 66).

During the 1950s and 1960s, air passenger traffic increased in volume by 15% per year, encouraged by increasing market demand and technological developments in aircraft design which increased the speed, range and passenger capacity of aircraft. Table 14 summarises these developments since 1940.

Table 12:
World Scheduled Domestic and International Air Traffic
(1974-1984)

Year	Number of passengers (millions)	% change	Passenger/ kilometres (millions)	% change	Load factor
1974	515	..	407,000	..	59
1975	534	3.6	433,000	6.4	59
1976	576	7.8	475,000	9.7	60
1977	610	5.9	508,000	6.9	61
1978	697	14.2	582,000	14.5	65
1979	754	8.1	659,000	13.2	66
1980	748	—0.8	677,000	2.7	63
1981	752	0.5	695,000	2.6	64
1982	764	1.6	710,000	2.1	64
1983	796	4.1	738,000	3.9	64
1984*	860	8.1	780,000	5.7	65

* estimates

Source: ICAO

Table 13:
Scheduled Traffic of Commercial Air Carriers:
Tonne-Kilometres Performed by Region (1979 to 1983)

ICAO statistical region of	Total Tonne-Kilometres Performed (Millions)					
	1979	1980	1981	1982	1983 prelim- inary	83/79 Variation %
Europe						
Total	43,010	44,755	46,935	46,870	48,785	13.42
Passengers	31,560	32,835	34,580	34,505	35,150	11.37
Middle East						
Total	3,840	3,925	4,220	4,625	5,390	40.36
Passengers	2,505	2,550	2,765	3,025	3,465	38.32
Asia and the Pacific						
Total	17,870	20,055	22,335	23,860	25,155	40.76
Passengers	12,750	14,175	15,645	16,555	16,875	32.35
Africa						
Total	3,215	3,540	3,930	4,085	4,220	31.25
Passengers	2,430	2,700	2,965	3,055	3,080	26.74
North America						
Total	52,535	51,455	50,305	50,955	54,215	3.19
Passengers	41,290	49,310	39,155	40,065	42,425	2.74
Latin America						
Total	6,395	6,980	7,310	7,280	7,150	11.80
Passengers	4,890	5,325	5,515	5,355	5,395	10.32
Total ICAO States	126,870	130,710	135,035	137,675	144,915	14.22
Passengers	95,420	97,895	100,625	102,560	106,390	11.49

Source: *ICAO Statistical Yearbook — 1983*

Note: 'Totals' indicate tonne-kilometres attributable to passengers, freight and mail.

'Passengers' indicate tonne-kilometres attributable to passengers and their baggage.

Table 14: **Aircraft Operational Characteristics 1940 to 2000**

Year	Type	Range (miles)	Speed (mph)	Capacity (seats)	Engine (type)
1940	DC-3	1,510	210	28	Piston
1950	DC-6	3,000	316	108	Piston
1960	B707	6,110	600	189	turbofan
1970	B747	7,090	608	350	turbofan
1980	Concorde	3,970	1,400	144	turbojet
1990	B747-400	8,000	620	414	turbofan
2000	B747-500	8,500	620	500	turbofan

Source: Travel and Tourism Analyst

In the 1980s, the impact of de-regulation on the US market and moves to liberalise air fares in the European and transatlantic markets, have meant that airlines need to be much more flexible in the face of changing consumer demand. However, current forecasts indicate that the passenger travel market will rise by about 5 per cent per annum up to the year 2000, when annual passenger movements will be rapidly approaching the 2 billion level.

There are over 7,000 aircraft currently in service in the world's airlines fleets, and about 40% of these are short to medium range aircraft with less than 125 seats, many of which, such as the BAC 1 – 11, are no longer in production. 25% of the world's aircraft are short to medium haul types carrying up to 185 passengers. The long-haul market, epitomised by the 747, accounts for 20%.

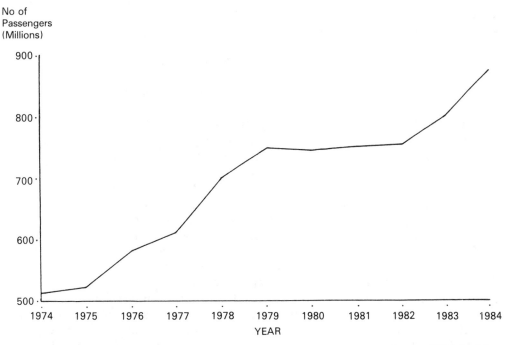

Figure 16: Growth in International Air Traffic 1974 – 84

Source: WTO Statistics

However, nearly 50% of the world's fleet is over 12 years old and some 2,000 aircraft (i.e. 28% of those in use) are approaching the end of their working life. Renewal of aircraft is now a major issue with many fleets, especially those in the less developed countries of Africa, South America and Asia. Table 14 below outlines estimates of expected aircraft requirements up to 1995.

Table 15:
Estimates of commercial jet aircraft requirements 1985 to 1995

Aircraft Manufacturer Type	Boeing	Airbus	McDonnell Douglas
Narrow bodies			
Short range	—	1,134	815
Short/medium range	—	1,719	1,347
TOTAL	2,560	2,853	2,162
Wide bodies			
Short/medium range	—	2,509	1,150
Long range	—	894	703
TOTAL	1,179	3,403	1,853
Overall Total	3,739	6,256	4,015
Assumed RPM growth (% per year)			

Source: *Flight International* March 15th 1986

The growth in traffic led to a growth in competition between airlines and they had to adapt fares and products to market needs to achieve better capacity levels in their aircraft. As Table 11 shows, load factors rose from 59% in 1974 to 65% in 1984 (seats sold as a percentage of seats available). One of the main means of increasing capacity levels has been to offer discounts in air fares for advance bookings (APEX, Advance Purchase Excursion or Super-APEX), seasonal discounts, and very competitive fly-drive packages with substantial discounts for car hire. All of these variations in pricing relate to scheduled services, and they have been very successful. However, the greatest increase in air traffic over this period has been in the air charter business, with the growth in inclusive air tours since the 1960s.

The tour operator prepares sample brochures for specific tours and then forwards this to one of the IATA member carriers (normally the one that will be used for the charter) for approval. The carrier then assigns an IT (Inclusive Tour) code number which must appear on the air ticket in order to qualify for the tour commission. Tour operators take advantage of the unsold capacity in existing aircraft owned by the airlines, who in turn wish to fill as many seats as possible and to avoid 'dead' legs on an airline route where few passengers may be travelling.

Charter Flights

The early charter flights in the 1960s took several forms because of existing regulations which limited the operations of charter carriers in Britain and the United States. There were the 'one stop inclusive tour charter' (OTC) the 'inclusive tour charter' (ITC) and the advance booking charter (ABC), as well as special interest 'affinity' groups which were set up simply as a means of obtaining low-cost air fares. The rules for these charters were constantly abused and ignored (especially for the affinity groups) since the government agencies regulating the operations of air carriers lacked the manpower to police them effectively. By the 1970s both the British and United States governments realised the in-effectiveness of these regulations and introduced less stringent regulations for air charters.

The pioneering firms in the tour operations business chartered aircraft on an *ad hoc* basis as part of a particular tour package that they put together, relying on a full aircraft to increase their load factor, reduce costs per passenger mile and thus dramatically lower air fares compared with scheduled services. Charter companies also reduce their operating costs by having fairly small numbers of administrative staff usually located in offices out of the city centre and will rely for the advertising and promotion to be handled by the tour operator and travel agent. Moreover, because they are not committed to operating a scheduled service, they can cancel flights at short notice if insufficient seats have been sold, or they can combine two flights on the same aircraft to make a flight viable. Scheduled flights will have precedence in using the main airports for departures and arrivals, so charter flights are often late at night or early morning, even for short haul routes. So although charter flights offer bargain fares, they do so with several strings attached. Charter traffic grew rapidly. In 1963 630,000 Britons were flying on inclusive charter tours; by 1971 this had increased to 2,482,000 and by 1981 to over 5 million. In 1987 over 8 million Britons are expected to take advantage of inclusive air charter tours.

There are now five main airlines flying charter package holidays mainly to the mass market destinations around the Mediterranean, and almost all using Boeing 737s for these short-haul flights. These airlines are:

(i)   Britannia Airways
(ii)   Orion Airways Ltd
(iii)   Air Europe
(iv)   Dan Air
(v)   Monarch Airlines Ltd

They normally fly from Gatwick and the main regional airports such as Manchester or East Midlands and the bulk groups of countries with an interest in a particular route. Outside of the schedule services, tour operators must also obtain a licence to operate inclusive air tours as a safeguard for passengers who could be stranded abroad if a company collapsed during the holiday season. The collapse of the aviation division of Court Line in August 1974 is a case in point, when 50,000 British holidaymakers were stranded abroad. (Dept. of Trade HMSO 1975). Package tour organisers must apply to the Civil Aviation Authority for an Air Travel Organisers Licence (ATOL) and the tour operator must provide evidence of financial viability as well as depositing a bond to meet the costs of repatriating passengers should the need arise.

To sum up, since 1945 the air transport industry has been regulated in three ways.

— at international level with IATA and the International Civil Aviation Organisation (a UN body);
— at national level by state control over fares and freight cargo rates offered to the public;
— bilateral agreements between governments covering specific routes, the number of flights on these routes, and the airlines who can fly them.

Although concern over safety standards and the financial viability of airlines is as strong as ever, there has been a general move during the 1980s to relax controls over fares, capacity, markets and frequency of flights in an effort to increase competition in the belief that market forces will create the best environment for air travellers. This move is referred to as 'de-regulation'. However, this raises the broader issue of the function of air transport. Is it a public service or a strictly commercial activity or a compromise between the two?

De-regulation

In the United States cargo de-regulation was introduced in December 1977 followed by passenger de-regulation in November 1978. Although this only affected internal domestic flights, the US began to negotiate de-regulated bilateral agreements for international services, coming into direct conflict with IATA which opposed complete de-regulation. Within the United States the whole regulatory system was further relaxed when the Civil Aeronautics Board was abolished in 1984. It is too early to predict the long-term impact of de-regulation in the United States, but it already appears to be having the following impacts on domestic air services:

— an expansion in small and medium sized regional and local airlines;
— more airline bankruptcies as competition intensifies;
— a growth in commuter services;
— fare wars;
— mergers between airlines in the face of increased competition;
— accelerated development of bub and spoke interchanges;
— commuter lines sharing code designations with larger lines?
— consumer services strained;
— 80 – 85% of all passengers flying on discounted tickets;
— one airline may dominate traffic into and out of one city.

In 1978 ten major carriers dominated US domestic traffic, accounting for 88% of the market share. By 1984, this group had shrunk to nine and their market share to 75%. Fifteen new airlines were started up, although they accounted for less than 5% of all traffic (Pryke 1987). Most of the newly certified carriers were located at secondary airports such as Midway, Chicago or Newark, New Jersey and many offered limited amenities, preferring to compete with low fares. One structural development that has emerged with de-regulation is the appearance of bus-and-spoke networks, with airlins increasingly basing their activities at a limited number of major airports.

The long-term effect may well be that although fares may drop in the short-term, the mergers will mean that much domestic traffic will be in the hands of a few large companies who will squeeze out the smaller operators. In Britain there has been increasing emphasis on competition between airlines and since 1983 talks have taken place within the European Economic Community to liberalise air fares throughout Europe, although this has met strong opposition from several national carriers and it will be a slow and gradual process.

At the international level the first moves to de-regulate air fares were initiated by the United States in the late 70s early 80s. Unfortunately, this was a period of rising costs and declining profits for all international airlines and this led to concerted opposition to whole sale de-regulation as airline financial losses were growing. The main problem with applying de-regulation internationally is that it affects national airlines of countries in different stages of development. Some countries may provide services as a means of generating foreign exchange, providing tourist access, as a national flag carrier, or to generate foreign trade and may not operate at a commercially viable level. Some of the developing countries come into this category and they may feel that they are unable to compete with the larger well-established international carriers based in Britain or the US.

However, the overall efforts to increase de-regulation on international routes are likely to continue, albeit slowly. One benefit of the increased competition created by de-regulation is that it forces airlines to be more efficient by scaling down their operations, improving productivity, improving aircraft load factors and improve their attractiveness to the traveller, particularly the business traveller.

Future Developments in International Air Travel

The major factors likely to influence international air transport are in the areas of aircraft technology, operations and distribution systems. Improvements in the operating efficiency of engines will help reduce fuel consumption as will the greater use of composite materials in airframe construction, together with more sophisticated flight systems which will make aircraft easier to fly. Estimates of operating costs vary, but the new generation of engines in use in the 1990s are likely to have cost savings 10% lower than existing versions. The main body of the Boeing 767 has only 3% composite materials but this gives it a weight saving of 630 kg, equal to the weight of 8 passengers. By 1992, composites such as carbon-fibre thermoplastics could cover up to 30% of the surface area of new aircraft, with corresponding savings in the payload cost. Improvements in on-board computers and display technology are likely to give volume savings of 60% and weight savings of 70% in the flight decks of the 1990s aircraft. Miniaturisation will also bring in small personal video screens for in-flight movies and individual passenger entertainment systems.

These technological advances will bring very real cost savings to those airlines who invest in the new aircraft types, and assuming that de-regulation produces a more liberal air transport environment worldwide, the airlines will be able to pass on these savings to their customers in the form of reduced fares, in order to maintain their market share. For example, Northwest Orient which has purchased up to 100 Airbus 320–200 aircraft, estimated that their fuel consumption will be 50% lower per seat than the existing fleet. This will enable the company to operate more effectively in a very competitive US market.

The increasing use of non-stop long range aircraft, such as the Boeing 747–400 first introduced by British Airways in 1989 is likely to give rise to strategic hub international airports similar to the pattern now emerging in the US domestic market. London, New York, Tokyo and Los Angeles are likely to emerge as world hubs.

ASSIGNMENT:

1. Outline what you consider to be the impact of de-regulation on:
    a) Domestic coach operations;
    b) Domestic air travel;
    c) International air travel.

2. Describe the impact of changing travel preferences on the traditional holiday resort.

Chapter 7

The Accommodation Sector

Learning Objectives: After reading this chapter you should have an understanding of:

— the main components of the accommodation sector;
— how these components operate;
— changes in accommodation preferences since 1970;
— the main companies in this sector;
— the distribution of accommodation in the UK;
— recent trends in this sector.

Introduction

In terms of jobs provided the accommodation sector is the major element of the tourist industry in Britain. Out of 1.5 million people employed in the tourist industry, 900,000 work in the hotel and catering sector. The growth in jobs in tourism between 1975 and 1985 was most evident in this sector with 270,000 out of the 325,000 new jobs created during that period. (English Tourist Board/Institute for Manpower Studies 1985). Between 1982 and 1985 while employment levels in the leisure and related services sector remained fairly static, over 92,000 jobs were created in the hotel and catering sector. So the accommodation sector has also demonstrated its resilience in times of economic recession and its ability to recover more quickly than many other tourism-related activities. Although these figures refer to the commercial accommodation sector it is important to have an understanding of all types of accommodation used and their importance to the tourist industry or the economy of a tourist region.

During the eighteenth and nineteenth centuries accommodation mainly consisted of coaching inns, boarding houses, and houses let for the 'season', with the emergence of 'grand hotels' following the development of the railways, when few major resorts were without at least one luxury hotel. The growth of mass tourism and the spread of holidays with pay saw the emergence of smaller hotels and boarding houses catering for the summer trade, and in the 1930s, the development of new types of accommodation including camping caravanning, youth hostelling and holiday camps. Post 1945 developments have included a mix of commercial activities such as villa holidays abroad, time-share holidays, consortia marketing country cottage or farm-house holidays; and non commercial activities such as visiting friends and relatives (VFR) and house exchange schemes, as well as the growth in the ownership of second homes.

Structure of the Accommodation Sector

The accommodation sector can be divided into two categories — commercial and non-commercial. In turn each of these has two components, the first is serviced accommodation; the second is self catering accommodation.

Commercial serviced accommodation is dominated by the hotel sector, and this accounts for 25 per cent of the tourist market in the UK. The types of companies operating in this sector cover the whole range from multi-national companies to franchises, cooperatives or sole owners. The Catering Intelligence Unit (CIU) of the Consumer Industries Press estimates that there are now 145 hotel groups in the UK operating 2,000 hotels with a total of 146,000 bedrooms. (Table .. on page ..) outlines the share of the British hotel market, and emphasises the importance of the international hotel chains. Two of the top three companies are US based, and have developed the system of *franchising* where the person operating the hotel pays a fee and royalties for using the brand name and marketing back-up of the parent company. Trusthouse Forte, Crest Hotels (owned by Bass PLC) Thistle Hotels (owned by Scottish and Newcastle), Holiday Inns and Ladbroke Hotels are the main companies with overseas interests. The Hotel Development Incentive Scheme (1969—73) which arose from the 1969 *Development of Tourism Act,* encouraged several companies with broad interests in leisure activities to invest in the tourist industry. Bass PLC acquired the Crest Hotel group; Scottish and Newcastle, The Thistle Hotels, and Ladbrokes have established their own hotel chains. Since the end of this scheme in 1973 few new hotels have been built. However,

Table 16:
Major UK Hotel Chains

Hotels operating in UK in Top 100	World Rank*	Total Rooms	Great Britain Hotels	Rooms
Holiday Inns	1	312,426	17	3,785
The Sheraton Corp	2	118,584	3	1,415
Ramada Inns	3	95,198	1	200
Trusthouse Forte	5	74,568	208	20,950
Marriott Corp	9	48,408	1	274
Novetel SIEH	11	46,253	5	1,088
Intercontinental	14	39,533	8	2,995
Hilton International	17	33,034	2	1,120
Hyatt International	23	13,826	1	228
Crest Hotels	29	12,220	54	8,184
Dunfey Hotels	36	10,929	1	800
Commonwealth Holiday Inns	42	9,648	—	—
Four Seasons	60	6,639	1	220
Penta Hotels	63	6,037	1	900
Thistle Hotels	78	4,963	39	5,952
Comfort Hotels	81	4,820	22	2,900
Taj Hotels	84	4,638	2	—
Ladbroke Hotels	86	4,600	32	3,500
Hotel Groups in UK				
Queens Moat			55	4,432
Mount Charlotte			43	5,300
Embassy Hotels			42	3,561
Swallow Hotels			31	3,000
Virani			19	2,200
Rank Hotels			5	2,074
Reo Stakis			24	2,000
De Vere Hotels			14	1,560
Norfolk Capital			10	1,000
Imperial Hotels			34	1,000
Metropole			5	2,000
Sarova			7	1,000
Seaco (Distinguished Hotels)			6	816
Savoy			4	636
Gleneagles			4	650

*According to the World's Top 100 Hotel Chains, prepared by Hotels and Restaurants Internationals.

the UK hotel market has remained fairly unchanged during the 1980s and faced with increasing competition for a share of this market a number of new companies have emerged as well as consortia of independent hotels who have combined their marketing operations. Examples of new Companies in the 1980s include the Queens Moat Hotels (55 hotels) and the Virani Group (19 hotels). The independent hotels who have formed marketing consortia have gained access to national and international markets through joint promotiuons. Table 17 shows the main hotel marketing consortia operating in Britain.

Table 17:
Hotel Marketing Consortia Operating in Great Britain

	World Rank*	Total Rooms	Great Britain Hotels	Rooms
Best Western	1	216,640	170	8,000
Leading Hotels of the World	7	44,000		
World Hotels	10	18,500		
Minotels	13	12,972		
Consort Hotels	20	5,000		
Exec Hotels	33	1,900		
Prestige Hotels	34	1,712	22	1,712
Guestacom	37	863		
Inter Hotels			103	n.a.

*According to the Top 37 International Consortia prepared by Hotels and Restaurants International.

The *self-catering sector* has grown in importance over the past 30 years at the expense of the unlicensed hotel and guest house sector. This includes rented accommodation, caravans, and tented camp sites. In 1957 15 per cent of British holidaymakers used self-catering accommodation and 31 per cent stayed in unlicensed hotels and boarding houses. By 1971 these proportions were reversed, and by 1981 over 36 per cent of Britons used self-catering accommodation on holidays in Britain.

Self-catering accommodation can take several forms. It can be:

— rented holiday flats, cottages or houses
— rented caravans
— rented tents
— holiday camps

Most of this self-catering accommodation is located on or close to Britain's coast, reflecting in part the long-standing preference for seaside holidays by most domestic tourists. The rapid growth and spread of coastal caravan and camping sites during the 1960s and 1970s gave rise to a range of conflicts and these are discussed in more detail in Chapter 12.

A recent study by the author of the Bournemouth and South East Dorset holiday region showed that there had been relatively little change in the proportion of serviced and self-catering provision between 1974 and 1984. Most of the self-catering accommodation is along a coastal strip within about half a mile of the sea. (Brown and Lavery 1987).

Farm-based accommodation has grown in importance over recent years as farmers have turned to other activities to supplement their income, and development grants have been made available through the tourist boards, notably the

West Country Tourist Board and the Wales Tourist Board. This accommodation may be serviced or self-catering. Accommodation in farm premises consists of rooms let either in the main building where the farmer and his family live or in another structure that has been converted from agricultural use to holiday accommodation. Letting of farm cottages is also popular, as is the development of small touring caravans or camping sites.

Although comprehensive and reliable statistics on farm tourism are not yet available, what is clear from the data that does exist is that in most EEC countries it has already established itself as an important element in the rural economy. Most of the information outlined below has been drawn from papers presented at the Marienhamn Symposium in 1982.

— *France*   There is a long tradition of farm tourism in France dating back to 1955 when the policy of *gites ruraux* was established. The amount of rural farm accommodation has almost trebled between 1973 and 1981 from 9,978 units to over 25,000. About 150,000 beds are provided in this sector with an estimated 7.5 million overnight stays.

— *West Germany*   Farm Tourism has a 12 year history in West Germany with almost 25,000 farms now offering tourist accommodation. Recent surveys by the University of Munich have shown that about 3 million West Germans are interested in spending their holidays on farms.

— *Ireland*   Farm tourism was developed in the early 1960s and the first listings contained only a few farm premises. The 1982 guide contains over 500 farmhouses offering tourist accommodation and a further 500+ farm cottages.

— *United Kingdom*   A conservative estimate suggests that 10,000 farms offer farmhouse accommodation and a further 10,000 offer self-catering accommodation. A further 5,000 farms provide camping and caravanning facilities.

— *Denmark*   To date (1979) only 500 farms provide for tourists and no capital grants are available. However, the marketing of farm tourism is heavily subsidised by the Danish Tourist Board who are also involved with the promotional literature.

No information is available on the extent of and growth in farm tourism among the other Member States of the European Economic Community. The summary report of the Marienhamn Symposium concludes that most of the farms depending on non agricultural income are interested in farm tourism (i.e. 40 to 60 per cent of all farms) and some regions particularly in Scandinavia show a very high growth rate in this activity. Farm tourism has not yet developed in Italy or Greece.

In the non-commercial accommodation sector visiting friends and relatives (VFR) is taking a growing share of the accommodation market. In 1961 visiting friends and relatives accounted for 32% of accommodation used. By 1980 this had increased to 43% of accommodation used by British Tourists. In the past the VFR market has been neglected as a segment of the total market but it is important also when marketing Britain to overseas tourists. In 1978 40 per cent of overseas visitors to Britain stayed with friends and relatives.

The growth in the ownership of private caravans and large trailer-tents has made self-catering mobile holidays available to a growing number of British holiday-makers. Membership of the caravan club of Great Britain increased by

40% 1950—1960 by 80% for individual and 221% for family members 1960—1980.

More recent trends include national and international home exchange schemes where for a small annual fee, individuals can exchange houses for the holiday period, and time-share developments where purchasers can buy exclusive use of a property for a specific period of the year. This development is discussed in more detail in Chapter 13.

Classification of Accommodation

There is no statutory registration systems for hotels in the UK although from January 1987 the National Tourist Boards for England, Scotland and Wales have introduced a new Crown Classification system. It covers *serviced accommodation* and will include all types of serviced establishments from listed for simple accommodation, to five crowns for top class accommodation. Previous attempts at voluntary classification were unsatisfactory because they relied on facts supplied by the owners/managers themselves without any checking. The new Crown system will ensure that no classification will be granted until a verification check has been carried out. Subsequent checks will be made on an annual basis. From 1987 onwards only those premises classified by the tourist boards will be included in their accommodation guides. The tourist boards hope that by introducing one scheme common to all serviced accommodation in Britain it will help the industry to market itself more effectively at home and overseas. By the end of 1986 over 10,000 establishments had been classified under this scheme.

The AA and RAC also operate their own classification schemes. Until the introduction of the Crown scheme the star rating awarded by the AA has been one measure of the quality of the serviced accommodation sector. Nearly 80% of the entries in the AA guide are in the 2 and 3 star categories — 6% are 4 star and under 1% are 5 star.

However, these systems of classifying or grading serviced accommodation are all voluntary unlike many European countries who have compulsory classification systems. With any voluntary system there will be many premises that, for whatever reason, choose not to apply for registration.

Problems Affecting the Accommodation Sector

The owner or manager working in the accommodation sector is working in a highly competitive commercial environment, and has to deal with several issues that can affect the success of his operation.

These include:

- the seasonality of hotel occupancy rates
- the cost and availability of manpower
- the supply of raw materials
- the availability of new technology
- interest rates and taxation policy

The domestic holiday market is still heavily concentrated in the period between June and August, and the accommodation sector faces the dilemma of gearing up to meet peak-season demand and then having under-used resources for the rest of the year.

To offset this seasonal peaking the British Tourist Authority introduced 'Operation Off-Peak' in 1972, with the aim of encouraging operators to put together development packages that would promote overseas visitor numbers during the trough periods — particularly the autumn and winter months.

During the 1970s organisations such as British Rail (see Chapter 6) and hotel consortia began to market short-break holidays outside of the peak period, and the growth in these has helped to improve hotel occupancy rates. Between 1977 and 1982 short holidays in serviced accommodation increased by 24% (BTA 1984).

In 1983 the Education and Training Advisory Council (ETAC) of the Hotel and Catering Industrial Board (HCTB) published a five-volume report on *Hotel and Catering Skills — Now and in the Future (HCTB 1983)*.

This report suggested that about 8 per cent of the workforce leave the hotel and catering industry each year and that with the growth in the accommodation sector there would be an overall shortfall of about 50,000 people by 1990.

New technology is playing an increasingly important role in the accommodation sector. A Gallup survey for the *Caterer and Hotelkeeper* in 1983 found that more than a third of hotels with 3 stars or more, regardless of size, possess computers. These are used for a wide range of functions including:

— Front office activities — reservations, accounting, ledgers, credit control;
— General office activities — financial control, day-to-day accounts, purchases, invoices, credit control;
— Room service accounting;
— Restaurant/meals and drink accounting;
— Telephone accounts.

Hotels that form part of a chain may have their activities linked by computer networks and the General Management/Boards of Directors can receive up to date information on the performance of individual hotels and consortia of hotels. Clearly staff working the front office or finance and accounting divisions of an hotel will have to have training in computer applications and usage, particularly data-base packages, viewdata systems and spreadsheets.

There is still a view in financial circles that hotels are a high-risk investment and this hampers the industry's attempts to raise sufficient quantities of capital particularly long-term capital. The government in their report *Action for Jobs in Tourism* (HMSO 1986) consider that it must be largely for the private sector to finance new hotel development (in London) and have asked the English Tourist Board to take the lead in discussing with financial institutions ways of improving the industry's access to private sources of capital. In addition the Regional Tourist Boards under the section 4 scheme can assist hotel developments which would otherwise not go ahead. In 1983/4 the English Tourist Board and the Regional Tourist Boards and local authorities approved £6.4 million in grants for hotel development/improvement schemes. Outside of London, the Urban Development Grant scheme is available to assist hotel schemes provided they meet the criteria for economic regeneration of deprived areas and provide a net increase in jobs and investment. The smaller hotel groups can also take advantage of the Business Extension Scheme which has been extended to cover existing businesses.

The Distribution of Accommodation in Britain

Serviced accommodation is concentrated in London and the main resort towns, although there has been a growth of new hotels around Heathrow and the major provincial cities. During the period 1971 to 1987 there was a significant decline in the number of hotels with less than 15 rooms, but little change in the overall number of hotel bedrooms available because of the trend towards large hotels with over 100 bedrooms.

London has the greatest concentration of hotel accommodation, accounting for over 17% of all rooms available in Britain. This reflects its pre-eminence as a tourist destination specially for overseas visitors. (In 1985 hotel occupancy in London was 78% compared with a national average of 67%.)

In the regions, the South West including the resorts of Torbay and North Cornwall, the South East (including Brighton, Eastbourne and Thanet, and Scotland) have the main concentrations of hotel rooms.

In terms of the domestic tourist market, the main concentrations of accommodation are associated with the large resort towns, although the growth of business trade and the development of purpose-built conference and exhibition centres has led to a growth of new hotels in cities like Birmingham and Manchester which are not normally considered 'resorts'. Indeed Manchester now has the largest stock of accommodation, in terms of bed spaces, outside of London.

Some hotel groups have moved into national prominence by buying up established hotels rather than seeking to build new ones. For example the Swallow Hotel Group, the North-East hotel chain owned by Sunderland brewers Vaux, bought a large London hotel in order to gain access to the London market. A recent trend has been for the independent hoteliers to form marketing consortia in order to achieve a market 'presence' at the national or international level. There are now at least 10 hotel marketing consortia operating in this way in Britain (Table 17 on page 75).

Recent Trends in the UK Accommodation Sector

The hotel sector has withstood the recession years quite well, by adapting to changing trends, identifying new markets, better market segmentation and more efficient management. The growth in the numbers of foreign tourists during the 1970s and 1980s has clearly helped the hotel sector, and the numbers of foreign visitors to the UK is expected to continue to grow during the 1990s. Hotels have begun to cater for the short break domestic market and most major chains offer special short break packages aimed at increasing occupancy levels during the shoulder and winter months. This pattern has increased dramatically during the 1980s.

Figure 17 shows the types of accommodation used by British residents on short break holidays (1 to 3 nights) and longer holidays (4 or more nights). It shows the three main types of accommodation used distinguishing between trips staying in hotels, other commercial accommodation, and staying with friends and relatives or using own caravan/second home. VFR (visiting friends and relatives) now dominates the short break market accounting for over two thirds of accommodation used 1982—1987. The hotel sector share is fairly static at 13% to 14%, but other commercial accommodation (42%) is more important for longer holidays.

Figure 17: Use of Commercial Accommodation on Holidays in England 1978-88

This chart shows the percentages of trips, nights and spending in England by main commercial accommodation types used on holiday in England. Length of column shows percentage in each accommodation. Numbers show estimated millions by volume and value.

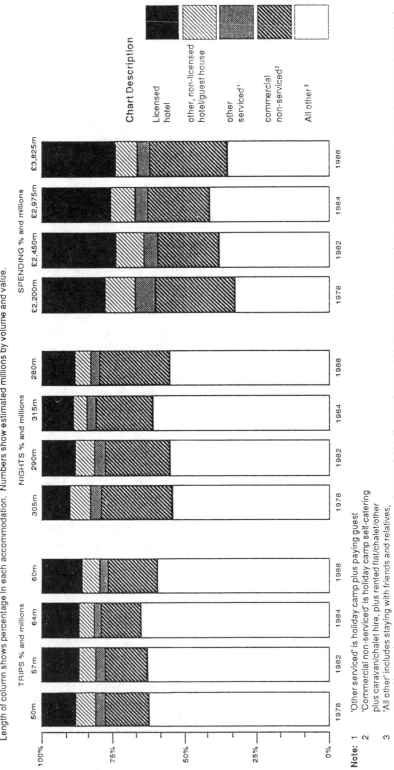

Note: 1 'Other serviced' is holiday camp plus paying guest
2 'Commercial non-serviced' is holiday camp self-catering plus caravan/chalet hire, plus rented flat/chalet/other
3 'All other' includes staying with friends and relatives, second homes, boats etc.

Source: British Tourism Survey. All holidays by adults and children accompanying them. 1984 data are on the new basis.

Spending on accommodation on holidays in England increased from £2,200 million in 1978 to £3,400 million in 1987 (English Tourist Board). As Figure 17 shows this increase in spending has mainly benefited the hotel sector, (an increase from £484 million in 1978 to £952 million in 1987) at the expense of the great house and holiday apartment sectors.

Holiday Camps

Another trend is for more people to go on holidays which do not need serviced accommodation. This was pioneered in the 1980s by entrepreneurs such as Billy Butlin and Fred Pontin, and by 1939 there were about 200 permanent camps scattered around the coast of Britain. During the 1950s and 1960s these holiday camps came to be concentrated into about 150 main centres and the majority are controlled by four major companies — Rank, Bass, Ladbrokes and Grand Metropolitan (now owned by Mecca Leisure).

Holiday Camp Operators	Number of centres	Beds
Butlins (Rank)	31	92,000
Pontins (Bass)	24	44,100
Ladbroke	18	31,000
Warner (Mecca)	14	10,500
	87	177,600

Source: *Euromonitor*

Table 18:
A Comparison of the Hotel Stock in Great Britain 1971/81

Hotels & boarding houses	1981 Units	Rooms	1971 Units	Room
Total Number	19,782	508,008	31,985	578,885
in region:				
North	888	22,216	1,900	33,370
Yorks & Humberside	1,113	25,638	1,450	22,360
North West	2,235	52,905	4,170	67,200
East Midlands	612	13,832	900	13,635
West Midlands	698	20,941	1,430	22,685
East Anglia	682	15,876	1,070	17,625
Greater London	2,174	88,084	2,495	72,845
South East (ex GLC)	3,195	78,467	6,740	121,885
South West	4,084	89,792	5,625	97,915
Wales	1,284	32,344	1,870	32,605
Scotland	2,727	67,913	4,335	76,760

Source: *Census of Population* 1981 and 1971

In the 1950s these holiday camps tended to attract a largely regional and working class clientele and their canteen-style catering and range of entertainments reflected this client group. The growth of cheap inclusive tours in the 1960s was aimed at this same market segment and the numbers of visitors to the holiday camps began to decline or fall off during this period. In response to this they have

Table 19:
**Trends in the Financial Turnover of the
British Hotel Industry 1974/1982**

	Hotels and Guest Houses	
	Current Prices £ million	Constant Prices 1980 = 100
1974	935	85.5
1975	1132	88.0
1976	1404	92.3
1977	1760	99.1
1978	2164	105.4
1979	2493	102.0
1980	2888	100.0
1981	3173	96.8
1982 estimate		95.2

Source: Catering Inquiry, DTI

changed their mode of operation, improved their range of amenities and aimed for a greater marketing mix. The emphasis is much more on self-catering based on small blocks of chalets or bungalows, with an image that is quite different to the traditional holiday camp of seaside chalets, bars and dance halls.

On the continent, a Dutch company have pioneered a new concept in holiday villages. The company is called Center Parcs (formerly Sportshuis Centrum) who started in the early 1970s as a chain of shops selling camping and caravan equipment. They have developed the concept of bungalow parks, usually set in a landscape of trees and lakes and focused on a large central complex of covered all-weather tropical pools. Water temperatures are around 25°C and they have wave machines, water shutes, saunas, solariums, bars and creches which are all part of the main pool complex. There are also a whole range of indoor and outdoor sports activities. There are now 8 sites in Holland and one in Belgium (Fig 18) and they are planning 6 developments in Britain by the mid 1990s. Two have now opened, the first at Sherwood Forest in 1988 and the second at Thetford in 1989. They are open all year round and have occupancy levels of over 95% over a 52 week period.

How do they do it? Well, clearly they have got the product right. The pool complex is the major attraction, particularly for families with children. They have gone for particular market segments for particular times in the year. So, outside of the main school vacation times they aim to attract families with pre-school children and older people who no longer have children. In Holland over 70% of bookings are repeat visits.

They also carry out regular surveys of their visitors to determine their likes and dislikes, and they have a special staff training programme for hospitality. In addition they advertise widely in newspapers, magazines and on the TV and radio. Another mark of a successful product is a large number of repeat visits and nearly half of their visitors are on repeat visits.

The concept of all-weather tropical environments with de luxe accommodation and a wide range of water-based recreation facilities appeals to several market segments and appears to be attracting new people to the bungalow park in considerable numbers. The additional appeal of these leisure complexes is that they can be enjoyed in all weathers and all seasons.

Figure 18: Distribution of Center Parcs in Europe

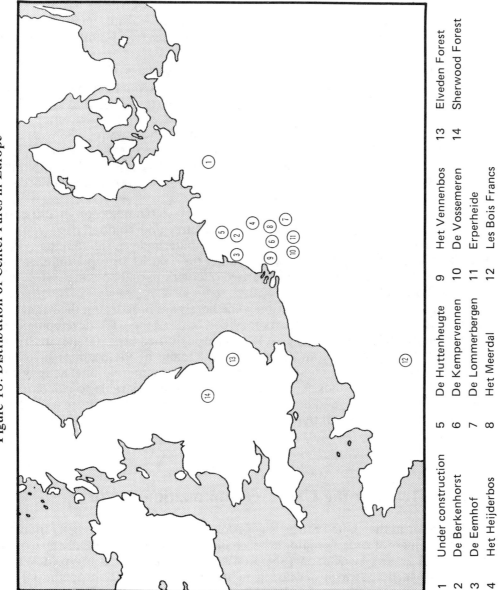

1	Under construction	5	De Huttenheugte	9	Het Vennenbos	13	Elveden Forest
2	De Berkenhorst	6	De Kempervennen	10	De Vossemeren	14	Sherwood Forest
3	De Eemhof	7	De Lommerbergen	11	Erperheide		
4	Het Heijderbos	8	Het Meerdal	12	Les Bois Francs		

Not content with their success in Holland, they have now invested £40 million in developing their first holiday park in England. Sherwood Forest about 100 miles north of London was chosen as their first site and was opened in 1988. They have now identified 2 further sites for bungalow parks. The second UK site to be developed was Thetford in East Anglia, in 1989. The Sherwood Forest bungalow park is focused on an all-weather dome complex containing swimming pools, waterfalls, whirlpools and waterslides. The holiday village has 600 stone-built villas in small clusters, set in 450 acres of trees, streams and a man-made lake. The luxury holiday village has a peak-season capacity of 3,000 and the first season operated at near full capacity.

In the face of this competition, and the evident success of Center Parcs, the Rank Organisation are spending over £40 million to redesign their Butlins holiday camps. Butlins at Minehead has been re-named Somerset World and £10 million was spent in 1985 to develop a water-leisure complex with enclosed water slides, new deluxe accommodation and a themed showbar. Bookings in 1986 were 30% up on 1985 and 60% up in 1987. The company plan to spend a total of £100 million over the next five years. Butlins at Skegness is to be remodelled on similar lines and re-named Funcoast World, and the camp at Bognor Regis will become Southcoast World.

One further development is the selling of resort accommodation in Britain in the same way as overseas holidays, with brochures and computerised booking systems. Five British resorts cooperated in a computerised central booking system known as WAVES. This is accessible through the Tourist Information Centres, and provided a comprehensive computerised reservations and booking system that is available to all hoteliers.

In the face of increased competition some hotels are broadening their range of functions to provide leisure or sports facilities, whilst others are developing conference business. The English Tourist Board has identified over 200 sites in Britain with development potential and is encouraging many of the traditional seaside resorts to invest in modern facilities. Tourism is now an international activity and if our accommodation stock is not modernised and comparable to standards in the best resorts overseas, and marketed imaginatively, it will lose its market share to new types of accommodation being developed.

Recent Trends in the USA Accommodation Sector

This sector in the United States is generally referred to as the lodging industry. The forerunners of today's major hotel chains were developed initially by Conrad Hilton and Ernest Henderson (Sheraton) followed in the post World War II period by Marriott (which developed in 1957 from a fast food operation) and Ramada founded by Marion Isbell also in the late 1950s. Each of the major chains was based on land ownership and they owned the land and buildings on which they operated, and managing a hotel was just part of a wider portfolio of real estate holdings, where if necessary the property could be sold and the cash generated then ploughed back into other hotels.

During the 1970s and 1980s companies such as Hilton Holiday Inn, Marriott and Sheraton expanded by selling off their real estate but retaining management contracts. This has enabled them to develop larger up-market hotels charging premium rates. Since 1980 new hotels with a total of over 700,000 rooms have been added. However, this rapid growth in hotel accommodation led to a temporary over supply with a decline in occupancy rates and profits for both independent hotels and the major chains.

Faced with this trend the major chain operators have begun to diversify their product and offer a wide range of accommodation types to different market segments of the travelling public.

As Table 20 shows, there are around 24,000 hotels in the USA almost evenly divided into chains and independent operators. The majority of the independent operators have under 300 rooms, with 30% having less than 75 rooms. These smaller hotels are mainly catering for the cheaper end of the market. In contrast only 19% of the chains operate hotels with under 75 rooms and 58% of the chains are hotels with 150 rooms or more.

Table 20:
The US Hotel Industry 1986

	Hotel Chains	Independent Hotels
No. of Properties	11,683	12,236
No. of Rooms	1,678,935	971,303
Number of rooms	%	%
Under 75	9.0	30.6
75 – 149	32.3	25.5
150 – 299	30.8	20.9
300 – 600	18.0	14.2
Over 600	9.9	8.2
TOTAL	100.0	100.0

(Source: Laventhol and Horwarth US Lodging Industry 1987)

One main trend between 1982 and 1986 has been the shift in location of the independent hotels with a 10% growth in resort locations whilst the chains show no significant difference between city centre, airport, suburban or resort locations. (Laventhol and Horwarth 1987).

An analysis of the market segments catered for between 1982 and 1986 shows that the independent US hotels have developed more business in the general tourism sector whilst the chains have seen a small growth in the business/conference market (Table 21)

The growth in numbers of incoming tourists since the mid 1980s due in part to the lower value of the US dollar, has greatly benefited the US hotel industry. The upturn in the domestic economy has also helped the domestic tourist industry and the general growth in incomes will encourage the spread of mini breaks and second or third vacations each year. All these factors will help improve occupancy rates and profitability in the US hotel industry. Laventhol and Horwarth estimate that there will also be a growth in new types of hotel and a general growth in the major chains at the expense of less successful hotel operators, either the small chains or the independents. Those hotels located in the sunbelt resorts with a good year-round climate should benefit from the general growth in the US travel and tourism market.

Table 21:
Market Share of US Hotels 1982 – 86

Market Segment	All	1982 Independent	Chain	All	1986 Independent	Chain
General Tourist	34.0	41.6	31.0	35.1	49.0	29.9
Business	44.2	37.8	44.9	38.8	27.5	44.0
Conference	15.7	15.3	17.6	18.1	17.1	18.2
Other	6.1	5.3	6.4	8.0	6.4	7.9
TOTAL	100.0	100.0	100.0	100.0	100.0	100.0

One of the most recent developments has been 'all suite' hotels. There are currently (October 1987) about 750 such hotels in the USA. According to the Laventhol and Horwarth survey these 'all suite' hotels are generating much higher occupancy levels than any other hotel product, and their attraction is that they can be designed to cater for a wide range of different market segments from the business traveller to the family on vacation.

ASSIGNMENT

Produce a proposal (for a major multi national company with a wide range of business interests) setting out:

a)   the optimum locations for accommodation development in Britain;
b)   the types of development.

Justify the reasons for your decisions.

Chapter 8
Public Sector Tourism

Learning Objectives: After reading this chapter you should have a clear understanding of:

— the main aspects of public sector tourism;
— the role of the Tourist Board;
— the development and future of public sector tourism.

Tourism is the mixed economy in action, and nowhere is this more evident than in the promotion of tourism where the public sector plays a major role. An important part of the promotion and marketing of individual resort towns and indeed of the UK as a tourist destination generally, is done by public sector bodies such as the National, Regional or Local Tourist Boards — yet the product being sold is largely run and owned by the private sector. Why is this? How has this come about?

There are at least five sound reasons why public sector bodies promote tourism:

(i)   it can make a significant contribution to overall economic activity of a country, region or town;

(ii) it can create new jobs;

(iii) it can make a significant contribution to the balance of income over expenditure — for a city, region or country.

(iv) synergy i.e. the working together of corporate organisations and regional/national bodies to produce an effect greater than the sum of their individual effects.

(v)   they can control the development of tourism by sponsoring projects in areas of high unemployment and by directing new developments away from environmentally sensitive areas.

The origins of public sector tourism in Britain can be traced back to the 'Come to Britain' movement which was founded in 1926 by Sir Francis Toule (British Tourist Authority 1975). Following a series of meetings in 1927 and 1928 between representatives of the Department of Overseas Trade, Members of Parliament and other prominent public figures, an organisation known as the Travel Association of Great Britain and Ireland was formed in April 1929 with a £5,000 grant from HM Government. The Association had two principal aims:

(a)   to increase the numbers of visitors from overseas to Great Britain and Ireland;

(b)   to stimulate the demand for British goods and services and to promote international understanding.

Within 12 months a 'Come to Britain' folder had been produced, giving information on tourist attractions, and coming events in Britain. In 1930 the Scottish Travel Association was established and it was agreed that they would supply the Travel Association of Great Britain and Ireland with information about Scotland and they would receive a grant from the parent body to promote tourism.

The public sector became more involved with promoting tourism following the Local Authorities (Publicity) Act of 1931 which enabled local authorities 'to contribute towards the cost of collecting and collating information in regard to the amenities and advantages of the British Isles or any part thereof, whether commercial, historic, scenic, recreational, curative or climatic, and of disseminating that information outside the British Isles provided that the expenditure did not exceed the amount which would be produced by the rate of one halfpenny in the pound levied at the rateable value of the area of authority'.

The Travel and Industrial Development Association faced the problems common to many industrial associations during the Great Depression of the 1930s, but by 1939 it had over 1,000 members drawn from the hotels and restaurants sector, the main rail and shipping companies and air and road transport firms. In 1938 over 720,000 overseas visitors had been attracted to Britain, spending almost £29 million — a figure which compared with the revenue from coal exports.

The most significant development in the years immediately after World War 2 was the decision to discontinue its industrial activities and concentrate on promoting travel to the UK and in 1946 the Board of Trade proposed the creation of a non-governmental organisation to develop tourist, catering and home holiday services.

In 1947 the government set up the British Tourist and Holidays Board (incorporating the Travel Association). This new body was the pre-runner of the present-day British Tourist Authority. The Board had 3 main objectives — to rebuild an effective tourist promotion organisation; to carry out market research and related studies; and to establish links with other national tourist organisations overseas. In 1948/9 the Board of Trade gave a grant of £326,500 to the Board and this marked an ongoing commitment to the involvement of the public sector in the tourist industry — a commitment that has remained constant over the intervening 30 years. The essential role of this organisation was summed up in 1950 when the British Tourist and Holidays Board and the Travel Association divisions were integrated to form the British Travel and Holidays Association. The Association was seen to have 2 main functions — bringing visitors from overseas to this country (the UK) and ensuring that they, as well as home holidaymakers, are well received and accommodated and have the best facilities that can be provided.

By 1960 the British Travel Association had offices in fifteen countries throughout the world and there were over 1.6 million visitors to Britain. During the 1960s several regional tourist associations were established with local authority support, including the London Tourist Board and the Lakes Counties Travel Association. However, these associations arose out of a voluntary approach towards developing tourism and it became increasingly clear that if a major expansion in tourism promotion was to come about central government must play a greater role.

Development of Tourism Act

The growth in the numbers of overseas visitors — over 5.8 million in 1969, spending £359 million — highlighted the potential of tourism as a creator of wealth and jobs. In 1969 the government issued the *Development of Tourism Act* which contained three main sets of proposals.

Part I established a statutory British Tourist Authority and Tourist Boards for England, Scotland and Wales with responsibility for promoting the development of tourism to and within Great Britain, and to encourage the provision and improvement of tourist amenities and facilities in Great Britain. The English, Welsh and Scottish Boards would have similar functions. In addition each National Tourist Board was given the authority to:

a) promote or undertake publicity in any form; and

b) to provide advisory and information services

c) to promote or undertake research.

The Act also enables the British Tourist Authority, after consultation with the English, Scottish and Wales Tourist Boards, to prepare schemes giving grant aid or loans to tourism development projects, which in the opinion of the Board would provide or improve tourist amenities or facilities.

The British Tourist Authority and likewise the English, Scottish and Wales Tourist Boards had the duty to advise any Minister or public body on any matters relating to tourism.

These Tourist Boards received their funding through the Board of Trade and the Chairman and members were appointed by the Board of Trade. So for the first time, after over 40 years of tourism promotion in Britain, the government established a national organisation with a statutory responsibility for the development and promotion of tourism in Britain.

Part II of the Act, which followed from an earlier White Paper on *Hotel Development Incentives* provided financial assistance for hotel development schemes. This assistance took two forms — grants and loans. Hotel Development Grants were available from the National Tourist Boards — but the hotel had to have at least 10 bedrooms (in Greater London 25 bedrooms) and the grant could only be claimed *after* the completion of the hotel. However, this provision meant that all small hotels were excluded from the scheme. Grants were also available for the extension or alteration of existing hotels, provided at least 5 additional bedrooms were added. The grants would meet 20% of the expenditure or £1,000 per bedroom, whichever is the less. In development areas this grant was increased to 25% of total expenditure.

The National Tourist Boards could make loans of up to £500,000 to provide new hotels or extend or improve existing hotels, and would generally lend up to 30% for new hotels and 50% for improvements to existing ones. These grants or loans were directed to the private sector, and were not available to local authorities.

At the time this Act was passed three-quarters of hotel rooms in Britain were over 50 years old and many lacked modern amenities. Before 1969 new investment in hotel development was very limited and confined to a few larger companies. In 1969 new hotel building was producing about 2,000 rooms a year for an annual investment of £15 million. Section I of the *Development of Tourism Act* led to a rapid growth in the hotel industry, and by 1973 over 70,000 additional hotel bedrooms and had been provided at a total cost of over £300 million, almost doubling the capacity of hotel accommodation. However, the bulk of these were in London and many of the old traditional resorts still lacked modern hotels. However, the Hotel Development Grants Scheme was terminated in 1973 and the Section 4 system of grants and loans has largely replaced it. The next section of this chapter discusses the Section 4 scheme in more detail.

Part III of the *Development of Tourism Act* enabled the respective Tourist Boards to maintain registers of accommodation and to introduce classification and grading of accommodation.

In the intervening years since 1969 there has been a massive increase in both international and domestic tourism. In 1969 Britain received over £350 million from spending by overseas visitors. By 1986 this had increased to over £5,000 million, and domestic tourism produced a further £6,000 million. A large measure of this growth is due to the efforts of the National Tourist Boards promoting Britain as a tourist destination and encouraging the development of tourism facilities and amenities throughout Britain.

ROLE OF THE TOURIST BOARDS

The British Tourist Authority

The main role of the British Tourist Authority is to promote incoming tourism to Britain. In order to do this it has established a worldwide network of 21 overseas offices and employs over 200 staff overseas. It has three primary objectives:

(i)   to increase visitor spending in Britain;
(ii) to increase and spread the overall level of travel beyond London to the regions of England, Scotland and Wales;
(iii) to extend the tourist season by promoting travel in the autumn and winter months.

The BTA works in partnership with the trade and other tourist interests and encourages support from the trade for their promotional work overseas. The BTAs overseas offices work closely with all tourist interests in the territories for which they are responsible who wish to market or commission travel products and holiday packages in overseas countries. This may include familiarisation trips and educational tours for overseas travel agents, tour operators and their sales staffs. They also run British Travel Workshops which bring together British producers with tourist services and products to sell and overseas buyers — travel agents and tour operators — who are keen to develop their business to Britain.

The English, Welsh and Scottish Tourist Boards

The three National Tourist Boards were all established in 1969 and each was given a remit to encourage tourists to visit and take holidays in their respective countries, and to encourage the provision and improvement of tourist amenities and facilities. Like the BTA all are financed by a grant-in-aid from central government. The Act also gave powers to the National Boards to establish committees to advise them in the performance of their functions and in the light of this the English Tourist Board created twelve Regional Tourist Boards to ensure effective coordination and cooperation on tourism matters at regional and local levels with local authorities and commercial operators. Figure 19 outlines the Tourist Board framework, and Figure 20 shows the distribution of Regional Tourist Boards in England.

Figure 19: Tourist Board Structure in Britain

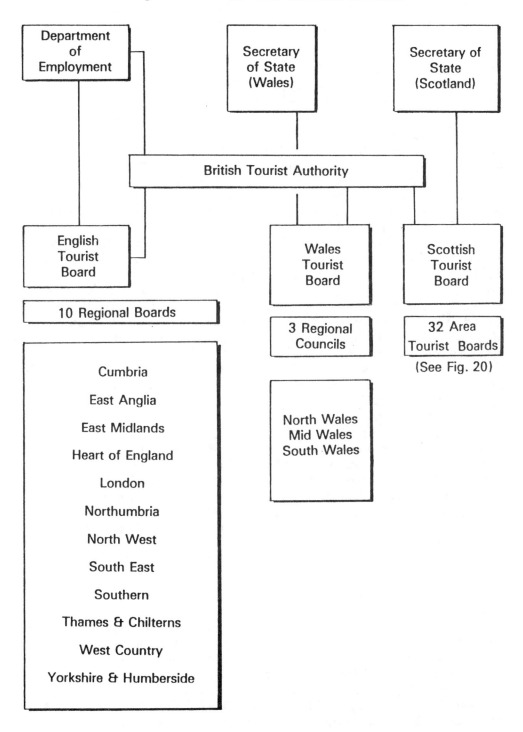

The English Tourist Board undertakes a wide range of marketing and promotional activities and one of its main campaigns is 'operation off-peak' aimed at extending the holiday season by promoting spring and autumn holidays. The ETB was empowered under section 4 of the 1969 *Development of Tourism Act* to give financial assistance for tourism development projects and in the financial year 1987/8 over £14.8 million was provided by the Board for tourism development projects. (ETB Tourism in Action July 1988). A very wide range of projects have been assisted by the Board ranging from hotel extension schemes to support for museum and theatres and countryside recreation projects. The Section 4 system funded two main categories of project. There was an *Innovation Fund* for projects costing over £100,000. The maximum grant was 20% of capital cost, given that the project has a significant tourism impact, was clearly viable, and clearly needed financial assistance. For projects costing over £100,000 ETB often inserted a clause making the grant repayable after a certain period of years provided that the business is sufficiently profitable. The major function of Section 4 funds was to act as seedcorn to encourage innovations and business expansion schemes that will benefit tourism generally.

On January 30th 1989 the Secretary of State for Employment who had ultimate responsibility for funding the English Tourist Board's operations, announced that the 'Section 4' scheme of financial assistance for tourism projects was to be suspended in England pending completion of a major review of tourism policy which began in 1988 in answer to a Parliamentary Question the Secretary of State pointed to the high levels of private sector investment where in England over £2 billion was invested by the private sector in major tourism and leisure projects during the first half of 1988 compared with £10 million in assistance through the Section 4 scheme in 1988/9. Clearly the Government felt that in the late 1980s the continuing high level of investment and confidence of the private sector in the tourism industry made it unnecessary to continue incentives through grants and loans.

The Wales Tourist Board, which is based at Cardiff has a similar range of services to the ETB, although there are just three Regional Boards for Wales.

The Scottish Tourist Board originally established nine Regional Tourist Boards (Figure 21) but by the early 1980s it was clear that such large Boards were too unwieldy given the distribution of population in Scotland and the distances between settlements in the North and West of Scotland. By 1983 the nine Regional Tourist Boards in Scotland had been replaced by 32 Area Tourist Boards almost completely covering the country.

The Regional Tourist Boards

The Regional Tourist Boards are autonomous bodies and draw their funding and membership from local authorities and commercial tourist operations within their areas as well as funding from central government via the English or appropriate National Tourist Board. They are autonomous commercial companies limited by guarantee. The constitution and internal organisation varies from Board to Board, as do the staff and financial resources. Many of the functions and operations of the Regional Tourist Boards are similar in kind if not in scale, to the National Tourist Board. A major part, therefore, of the Regional Tourist Boards activity is focused on the marketing and promotion of their own region.

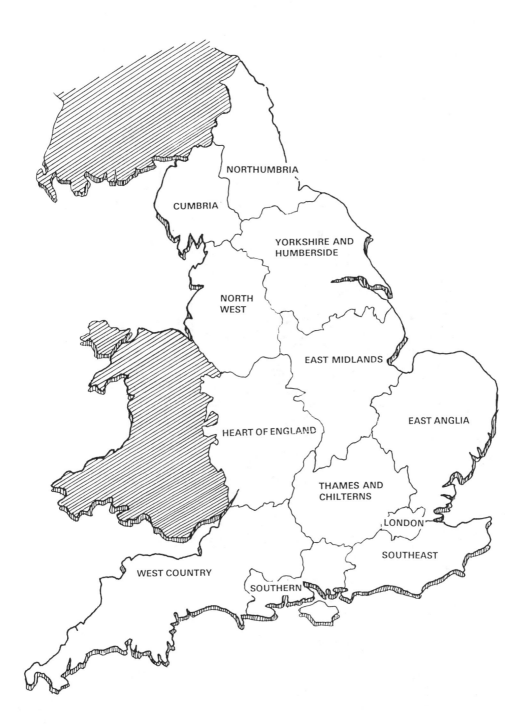

Figure 21: Scotland's Area Tourist Boards

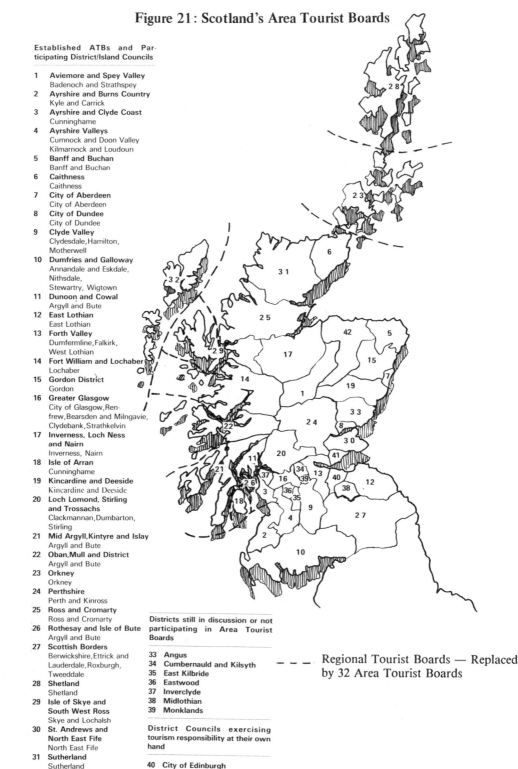

Established ATBs and Participating District/Island Councils

1　**Aviemore and Spey Valley**
　　Badenoch and Strathspey
2　**Ayrshire and Burns Country**
　　Kyle and Carrick
3　**Ayrshire and Clyde Coast**
　　Cunninghame
4　**Ayrshire Valleys**
　　Cumnock and Doon Valley
　　Kilmarnock and Loudoun
5　**Banff and Buchan**
　　Banff and Buchan
6　**Caithness**
　　Caithness
7　**City of Aberdeen**
　　City of Aberdeen
8　**City of Dundee**
　　City of Dundee
9　**Clyde Valley**
　　Clydesdale, Hamilton,
　　Motherwell
10　**Dumfries and Galloway**
　　Annandale and Eskdale,
　　Nithsdale,
　　Stewartry, Wigtown
11　**Dunoon and Cowal**
　　Argyll and Bute
12　**East Lothian**
　　East Lothian
13　**Forth Valley**
　　Dumfermline, Falkirk,
　　West Lothian
14　**Fort William and Lochaber**
　　Lochaber
15　**Gordon District**
　　Gordon
16　**Greater Glasgow**
　　City of Glasgow, Renfrew, Bearsden and Milngavie,
　　Clydebank, Strathkelvin
17　**Inverness, Loch Ness
　　and Nairn**
　　Inverness, Nairn
18　**Isle of Arran**
　　Cunninghame
19　**Kincardine and Deeside**
　　Kincardine and Deeside
20　**Loch Lomond, Stirling
　　and Trossachs**
　　Clackmannan, Dumbarton,
　　Stirling
21　**Mid Argyll, Kintyre and Islay**
　　Argyll and Bute
22　**Oban, Mull and District**
　　Argyll and Bute
23　**Orkney**
　　Orkney
24　**Perthshire**
　　Perth and Kinross
25　**Ross and Cromarty**
　　Ross and Cromarty
26　**Rothesay and Isle of Bute**
　　Argyll and Bute
27　**Scottish Borders**
　　Berwickshire, Ettrick and
　　Lauderdale, Roxburgh,
　　Tweeddale
28　**Shetland**
　　Shetland
29　**Isle of Skye and
　　South West Ross**
　　Skye and Lochalsh
30　**St. Andrews and
　　North East Fife**
　　North East Fife
31　**Sutherland**
　　Sutherland
32　**Outer Hebrides**
　　Western Isles

Districts still in discussion or not participating in Area Tourist Boards

33　Angus
34　Cumbernauld and Kilsyth
35　East Kilbride
36　Eastwood
37　Inverclyde
38　Midlothian
39　Monklands

District Councils exercising tourism responsibility at their own hand

40　City of Edinburgh
41　Kirkcaldy
42　Moray

– – – Regional Tourist Boards — Replaced by 32 Area Tourist Boards

Scottish Tourist Board Annual Report

Activities will include the productions of regional accommodation/facilities guides, advertising campaigns, exhibitions and workshops. Most Regional Boards receive their main source of funding from commercial revenue-earning activities such as selling space, consultancy activities and so on. Table 22 shows the percentage of income from such activities compared with their subvention from the National Board.

Table 22: Regional Tourist Boards Sources of Income

	English Tourist Board Subvention	Local Authority %	Commercial Membership	Other*	TOTAL
Cumbria	23	14	13	50	100
East Anglia	22	12	7	59	100
East Midlands	30	15	6	49	100
Heart of England	22	20	14	44	100
London Visitor and Convention Bureau	19	-	44	37	100
Northumbria	23	48	5	24	100
North West	17	15	4	64	100
South East	26	19	12	43	100
Southern	15	9	6	70	100
Thames & Chilterns	22	4	12	62	100
West Country	18	13	11	58	100
Yorkshire & Humberside	21	25	8	46	100

* ("Other" includes selling space, advertising revenue, consultancy, etc)

SOURCE: English Tourist Board Annual Reports.

The Regional Tourist Boards are closely concerned with the network of Tourist Information Centres throughout Britain (TICs) and generally provide the local contact and distribution for the Boards. In some instances, particularly the more important tourist destinations, the Regional Tourist Boards also provide and staff limited number of centres to complement those provided by the local authority.

The Regional Tourist Boards were also responsible for the local administration of the Secton 4 grant aid scheme for capital projects. Initial applications for assistance were made to the Regional Tourist Board who advise the ETB on particular applications. The Regional Boards had the delegated authority to recommend for approval grants of up to £100,000 for tourism development projects, although the actual decision-making authority still rests with the English Tourist Board.

A major role of the Regional Tourist Boards is the provision of development advice to commercial operators within their area, and liason and advice on tourism planning and management matters with local authorities. As well as disseminating information about surveys undertaken by the National Tourist Boards, the Regional Tourist Boards also undertake their own surveys and research to provide more detailed local information.

Each Regional Board is also responsible for the preparation and development of tourism strategies for their regions. These will be generally coordinated with strategies prepared by other bodies concerned with tourism and recreation such as the Countryside Commission, the Sports Council, the Association of District Councils and so on

The Regional Tourist Boards have the advantage of both local authority sup-

95

port and backing from commercial tourism operators, and are therefore in a strong position to help individual local authorities in preparing inputs to local structure plans, expressing comment on applications for tourism developments, and providing advice and information during the consultation and submission stages of major plans, which affect the Travel and Tourism Industry.

Local Authorities and Tourism

At the most local level many local authorities are directly involved with the tourism industry in a variety of ways. Often they own and manage facilities that are major tourist attractions such as museums, theatres, country parks or historic monuments. They often have their own tourism officers or recreation and leisure officers who include tourism in their remit. All the major resort towns have their own publicity and promotion units either in the Town Hall or in the borough's tourism department. They often set up and run the tourist information centres, manage camping and caravan sites, the beaches and the seafront areas. Some local authorities such as Bournemouth, Brighton and Harrogate, have built large conference centres to promote and encourage business tourism. Often these facilities — such as the Bournemouth International Centre — are also designed as venues for major sporting events and festivals.

The first priority of local authorities is to provide a range of leisure and cultural facilities for local residents. These will vary from outdoor facilities such as playing fields, parks and gardens, golf courses, country parks and picnic sites, to indoor facilities such as sports centres, leisure pools, museums, art galleries, theatres and concert halls. All of these facilities and their related infrastructure of car parks and amenities, will also attract tourists and will be used by them.

Local authorities also often provide indirectly for tourism by contributing to the income and work of the Regional Tourist Boards, and by giving planning permission or grants-in-aid to tourism development projects. No two local authorities are exactly alike in the way tourism is developed or promoted, and the importance of tourism in the local authority's policy plan will vary depending on whether tourism is perceived as being of value to the local economy. In the early 1980s it was estimated that local authorities were responsible for over 500 art galleries and museums, 700 indoor swimming pools, 600 indoor sports centres and 200 golf courses.

The local authorities provide and resource these facilities in a variety of ways. The public has free access to beaches, picnic sites, country parks, nature trails and so on, and whilst the public doesn't pay directly for these facilities it does so indirectly through the rates. Local authorities also provide other facilities such as leisure pools, marinas and golf courses where there is a direct payment by the user although this is often highly subsidised.

That tourism is the mixed economy in action is best demonstrated by the major British seaside resorts. Much of the advertising, marketing and general promotional activity is done directly by the local authority, although it is the private sector in the form of hotels, guest houses, coach operators and tourist attractions that benefit from this.

Local authorities spend a considerable amount of money — in excess of £500 million on sport and recreation facilities and about £80 million on cultural activities, shared equally between museums, galleries and theatres. Much of this spending goes on staffing existing resources, although some of it is used for a wide range of grants to voluntary bodies working in the tourism and recreation sector.

As planning authorities they can assist tourism development projects by making land and/or resources available. They can also give planning approval to private sector tourism developments where they are seen to be for the general benefit of the town or region. Local authorities have very wide discretionary powers and by channelling resources to tourism and recreation they can have a major role to play in developing a town or region as a tourist destination.

Between 1984 and 1987 district councils spent over £521 million on tourism-related projects and over 10,000 new jobs were created both directly and indirectly as a result of this investment. Over the past decade many local authorities, in association with Tourist Boards and various other agencies have developed tourist facilities based on their cultural, industrial or historic heritage. For example Torfaen Borough Council in association with the Welsh Development Agency, the Wales Tourist Board and the National Coal Board developed the Big Pit Mining Museum. Portsmouth has developed a range of attractions based on the theme of maritime heritage with HMS Victory, HMS Warrior and the Tudor warship, Mary Rose, as the centrepieces of a formal Royal Dockyard. The city is now embarking on a major development programme with a £5 million water recreation centre; a £100 million marina and a £100 million indoor shopping centre.

Local authorities have also begun to realise the advantages of coming together to establish marketing consortia with the common aim of increasing their region's share in the domestic and international tourist market. For example, Devon, Somerset, Torbay, Exeter and Plymouth have formed a consortium to attract more U.S. visitors to the south west of England. Several local authorities combined to promote nationally the Great English City Break campaign.

The Future of Public Sector Tourism

In the mid 1980s the government adopted a higher profile in tourism policy and with the report *Pleasure, Leisure and Jobs — the Business of Tourism* (HMSO 1985) it outlined the growing importance of tourism in the UK economy and suggested ways in which obstacles to the industry's faster growth might be removed. In September 1985 responsibility for tourism policy in England and for Great Britain as a whole was transferred from the Department of Trade and Industry to the Department of Employment which is a much larger ministry, thus giving tourism policy makers access to more finance and resources.

Both BTA and ETB were asked to give particular attention — in both marketing and development programmes — to encouraging tourism in areas of the country with untapped tourism potential and higher than average levels of unemployment, and to extending the tourist season. The government provided a 20 per cent increase in grants-in-aid and Section 4 support giving a combined total of £40 million for 1986/7. Much of this funding is being directed at new initiatives such as highlighting the tourism potential of inner city areas (*Action for Jobs in Tourism* HMSO 1986).

As a means of encouraging greater local authority commitment to the development of tourism in their areas as well as better links with the private sector, the

Figure 22: Funding for tourism projects 1986

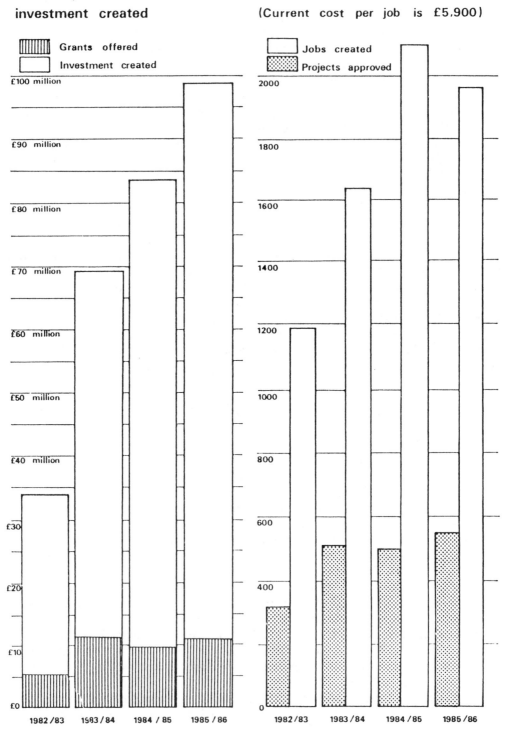

English Tourist Board has introduced a series of *Tourism Development Action Programmes*. A Tourism Development Action Programme consists of a package of development, marketing and research initiatives which can be implemented rapidly, and is usually a partnership between the local authority, the English Tourist Board, the Rural Development Commission and other agencies. They concentrate on initiatives that can be achieved in the short-term and usually operate for a limited duration of up to two to three years. Tourism Development Action Programmes are currently in progress in Bristol, Bradford, Portsmouth and Tyneside and the rural areas Exmoor and Keilder now have TDAPs. Over £40 million will be spent on these developments. In 1987/8 the English Tourist Board launched six new TDAPs: the Isle of Wight, Forest of Dean, Norwich, Carlisle, Shropshire and Lancaster and have a target of 20 active TDAPs by 1990. To widen the scope of these tourism development action programmes, the English Tourist Board has involved other agencies, wherever appropriate, to be full partners in these action programmes.

The seaside resorts of Torbay and Bridlington have been given special funding for comprehensive marketing and development strategies and were selected following a 'Resorts 2000' competition organised by the English Tourist Board.

Finally, the English Tourist Board has given an unprecedented £1.5 million grant offer to the Dutch-based company Centre Parcs Ltd. towards the construction of an all-weather all-year holiday complex at Sherwood Forest. Clearly, public sector tourism is thriving and is often taking the lead in supporting innovative tourist developments.

In 1987 the English Tourist Board gave £14.84 million in Tourism Development Grants to over 600 projects. These cash injections generated £117.5 million of investment and created 2,800 full-time jobs. (*Tourism in Action*, July 1988). A further £3.8 million in grants was given to 481 small business projects costing under £100,000 from the Business Development Fund.

The review of the English Tourist Board's functions was completed by the summer of 1989. This resulted in proposals to scale down much of ETB's activities and to devolve many initiatives to the regional tourist boards with effect from April 1990. These include:
- virtually all the ETB's local development work such as tourism development action programmes;
- operational responsibility for accommodation grading scheme;
- responsibility for tourist information, including development of the network of the tourism information centres;
- local marketing and the encouragement of training

In addition other ETB functions will be privatised or phased out in line with the government's "streamlining" policy announced by the employment secretary in July 1989. Among the key functions to be privatised or contracted out include the promotion of trade events and the production and publication of accommodation guides.

The effect of these changes will be to reduce the ETB staff compliment by one-third, and the loss of so many experienced and qualified staff over such a short time span could have a very detrimental impact on public sector tourism at national level in the 1990's. The abandonment of the Section 4 grants scheme will be particularly felt by many small tourism businesses in the regions who relied on

ETB grants and loans to upgrade and improve their facilities and gear up to meet the challenge from abroad.

ASSIGNMENTS

1. The South coast resort of Seamouth has a tourism infrastructure that dates back to its Victorian heyday. Since 1945 it has had a gradual decline in visitor numbers and has become better known as a retirement area than as a tourist resort. There has been little investment in its tourist industry over the past 40 years.

    You have been appointed as a consultant to undertake a feasibility study into the prospects for reviving the tourism industry in order to attract jobs and investment into the local economy. Show how this can be done, taking advantage of the Regional and National Tourist Board network, and suggest what changes are needed to improve the management of the resort at a local authority level.

2. You are a Senior Civil Servant and have been asked to produce a memorandum for the Minister with special responsibility for Tourism, setting out how public sector tourism should be re-organised and developed in Great Britain.

    Using *NO MORE THAN* 3 sides of A4 outline and justify your proposals.

Chapter 9

Planning and Development of Tourism

Learning Objectives: After reading this chapter and the references contained in it, you should have a clear understanding of:

— the role of both the public and private sector in planning for tourism;
— the stages involved in preparing a feasibility study of new tourism developments;
— the financing of tourism developments;
— the main elements in the tourism planning process.

Introduction

Historically, many interests — both public and private — have played a part in the development and provision of facilities for tourism. This has ranged from the parks, promenades and piers of the Victorian period, to the hotels, leisure complexes and conference centres of the present-day. This planning and development was generally influenced by speculative developers and entrepreneurs up to the 1930s, but after the 1947 Town and Country Planning Act local authorities for the first time were given wide powers to control the development of public and private land and facilities in towns and countryside.

As tourism grew in scale during the 1930s, and increased rapidly with the advent of mass tourism in the post-war years, this brought with it the recognition that the tourist resources of the community and region needed to be managed so as to reconcile conflicts over the use of land, so as to plan to meet future needs, and to create an environment within which tourists could enjoy both natural and man-made resources without damaging or destroying the very features that attract them in large numbers.

The second decision that both private and public sector organisations must make is to compare the supply of tourist resources (both natural and man-made) with the demand for them, in order to identify short-falls in provision. A public or commercial organisation will require an inventory of the supply and distribution of tourist facilities in order to identify potential for tourism development. *Demand* can be defined as the use of existing tourist facilities and the desire to use them either now or in the future. The people who take part in tourist activities make up the *effective demand*. In addition there is the *deferred demand* (that is those who could take part in domestic or overseas tourism, but do not, either through lack of knowledge or lack or facilities or both); and *potential demand* (that is, those who cannot at present participate and require an improvement in their social and economic circumstances to do so).

Tourism Development (Project Appraisal)

Having identified a market, chosen a site, obtained clearance for building and funding for the project, there is a need for the national, regional or local govern-

101

ment to assess the impact of tourism developments. Tourism projects cannot be planned independently because they have a wide range of impacts on the cultural, physical and economic environments of the locality. Physical planning (i.e. land use planning) is important as a means of organising the distribution of facilities, the conservation of natural resources and the integration with other sectors of the economy. The *scale* of tourism developments is a critical factor and one that will have the most immediate impact on the environment. This issue is discussed in more detail in Chapter 12.

At National or Regional level the first strategic decision is whether to concentrate developments in those regions or localities which are accessible and most likely to attract tourists, or to disperse facilities so as to ensure that as many areas as possible benefit from tourism developments. Concentrating development projects provides economies of scale, but raises problems of environmental impact.

There is a need to study the effects of new facilities on usage rates from within their catchment area. Supply of new facilities may transform latent demand into effective demand; and bring changes within the pattern of effective demand. The degree of substitution between one kind of facility and another should be measured, and depends on the inherent attraction of different tourist resources in relation to centres of demand. The 'drawing power' of tourist resources is linked to individual perception of tourist facilities or landscape resources and the motivation of tourists.

It is essential to have a tourism development plan in the following situations:-

(i)   in regions that cater for mass tourism;
(ii)   in regions with a fragile natural environment;
(iii) in newly-developing tourist regions.

One of the paradoxes of mass tourism is that in particular cases tourists by arriving in large numbers may cause overcrowding and congestion which can destroy the very thing they come to see. In any tourist region there is likely to be a range of development opportunities and a series of thresholds for development. Thus for areas that have fragile environments which make them highly sensitive to visitor numbers, access has to be discouraged. Areas that are scenically attractive which are wild and relatively remote should have limited vehicular access. Areas suitable for intensive tourist use should be identified and developed so as to absorb visitors. Development Planning operates at three different levels — national, regional and local. At the national level the National Tourist Board produces strategic plans (usually on a 4 to 5 year basis) which set out the broad framework within which all the agencies involved in tourism can coordinate their activities. This document usually outlines investment plans and policy decisions in tourism development. For example in its document *Strategy for Growth 1984 — 1988* (BTA 1984) the British Tourist Authority reviews the trends in tourism to Britain 1972—1982 and identifies the main strengths and weaknesses of the British market. It then identifies economic and social factors and government policies likely to affect tourism over the plan period. The document concludes by identifying, in the light of BTAs objectives, the target markets and new product development required to translate this strategy into action.

At the regional level the Regional Tourist Board will produce a coordinated strategy for tourism and this is usually implemented through a Development Panel consisting of both local authority and private sector interests who are members of the Tourist Board. The final part of this chapter outlines two case studies which demonstrate the planning and development process.

Planning for Tourism

In this context, what does 'Planning' mean? It means several things, and attempts to be an amalgam of the best of them. For the public sector it means reconciling conflicts over the use of land. In the case of both private and public sector organisations it means managing resources effectively (both natural and man-made) so that the best use is made of scarce resources. It means identifying features or sites with tourism potential and preparing proposals to develop them to meet an actual or predicted demand. Planning is concerned with relating the supply of tourist facilities to the demand for them, so that public needs are met without under or over-provision. Planning can be pro-active in initiating tourism projects, and should not be seen as a negative approach associated with controls, regulations and restrictions. Planning has increasingly been seen as a means of safeguarding the environment from excessive or ill-thought out tourism development, and there are now several public and quasi-public bodies with an interest in and responsibility for land management. Planning should be a partnership between the public and private sector and in recent years there has been a trend towards more public-private partnerships epitomised in the Tourism Development Action Plans which involve assembling large parcels of land and complex financial packages and creating opportunities for large-scale private investment in tourism projects.

These projects are not only focused on urban areas, but in the countryside also. The 10 national parks and stretches of heritage coast around Britain (Fig 7 on page 27) represent major tourist resources identified over the past 40 years. During the 1960s and 1970s it was recognised that the network of national parks was not sufficient and many country parks were developed around all the major towns and cities, with the aim of encouraging more people to enjoy and use the countryside on their doorstep.

Planning for tourism raises issues related to *resources* and *management*. Resources can be natural (forests, lakes, beaches, scenery) or man-made (theatres or visitor centres) or the financial investment needed to translate plans into reality. Management covers management policy and management action both in the provision of tourist facilities and their day-to-day operation. In other words, the provision of facilities is not enough. They must be managed efficiently so as to maximise the public's use and enjoyment of them whilst ensuring that the public organisation or private business covers its operating costs.

Both the public and private sector have a common approach towards managing tourist facilities. Both are concerned about value for money and effective control of budgets and looking at ways of maximising their income over expenditure. The growth of public and private sector partnerships suggests that each sector needs to understand how the other operates and to share management skills. Usually the major professional bodies such as the HCIMA or the Tourism Society draw their members from both sectors.

The public and private sector should have similar, if not identical, approaches towards preparing proposals for new tourism developments. Five main factors need to be considered when preparing a feasibility study for new tourism facilities;

The Market

The principles and practice of tourism marketing are discussed in more detail in Chapter 10, but it is sufficient to say that in planning any tourism project several questions need to be asked:

— what is the target market?
— what facilities/features will attract them?
— is it a growing or declining market?
— how much will people pay to use the facilities?
— how can this market be reached?
— what competing facilities exist and what are their objectives and weaknesses?
— what is the planned capacity?
— what is the planned 'season'?

The answers to these questions can be found by undertaking detailed market research and this is discussed in the next chapter.

The Location

What is the best location for a new tourism development? Clearly this depends on the type of facility being provided and whether or not it needs to be adjacent to a lake, river or the sea. Should it be near a major concentration of population or in a quiet country area? Accessibility is usually a key factor because unlike other products, the tourist product has to be consumed on the spot and potential customers need to be able to travel to the facility quickly and inexpensively. Is there good road, rail and air access? Does it need to be located adjacent to other tourist resources?

Having identified a location, the next step is to select a site for the development. Is it an established tourist area, or is it a new area with tourism potential? What is the local authority or government policy towards this kind of tourist development?

The Site

At this stage planning issues need to be carefully considered. Does the site have planning permission for the land use proposed? If not, can this permission be obtained or will there be planning constraints on the site? Are there mains services available or if not, can they be provided? Is the site accessible from the main road? Will the development require extensive landscaping works? is there sufficient land to provide adequate car parking? Is there room for expansion on the site should the development be very successful? All of these factors need to be considered when the developer applies for outline planning permission, which is the first stage in getting a project approved. This work would lead to an outline site plan, building elevations and sketches showing the main land use layout with details of the function of buildings and range of services to be provided.

The Management Structure

This is a critical element in deciding how a business is to be run and what it will cost to operate. How many permanent and how many seasonal staff will be needed? What tasks will each staff member do? What specialist skills will be needed? Will they have to be recruited nationally or locally? Will a staff training programme need to be developed? A typical management chart for a public sector and commercial sector organisation would probably have a senior management group above the facility manager, and in turn the senior managers responsible to Chief executives and council committees or boards of directors. At the facility level the main management activities will be planning and forecasting, budgetary control, dealing with the public, organising work, recruitment selection and staff training, working computerised systems and industrial relations.

Financial Appraisal

This follows from decisions about the type of tourist facility to be provided and the range of markets to be served. Very often the financial appraisal will include several forecasts based on a range of assumptions about the management of the project and changes in the financial climate. The assumptions must be based on accurate estimates of the capital cost of the project, the potential operating cost, and the potential revenue. A further factor is the degree of 'risk' if the project is providing a new form of tourist facility, related to the level of capital investment required and the rate of return on capital that can be earned. The element of 'risk' operates at two levels. First, the break even point below which the business will not survive. Secondly, the break even point beyond which investors will get a return on their investment. Potential guarantors will need to have this information. This will need to be set against a time scale which allows for the facility to come into full operation, to build up a 'market' and to produce actual as against forecasted accounts.

Financing Tourism Projects

(a) Public Sector Finance

In the public sector finance for tourism projects can be classified under two main headings. *Capital* finance and *revenue* finance. Capital spending is generally financed through borrowing approved by central government and is divided into two categories — key sector and non-key sector projects. The key sector developments reflect national policy or for example maintaining maximum standards for roads, hospitals etc and is controlled by agreement with central government departments. Tourism projects are non-key sector and here the local authority has a block allocation each year to be spent as it wishes. Many local authority services such as housing, education and the social services will be competing for this money. In addition local authority capital expenditure can be funded in several ways:

— direct government grant (e.g. Countryside Commission, or English Tourist Board (Section 4) grants from the regional or national tourist board);
— revenue contributions to capital spending (i.e. from the rates);
— capital receipts from the sale of local authority land;
— loans from commercial concerns;
— income from other sources such as lotteries.

Revenue finance comes from four main sources:

(i)   from the users of facilities (income from membership fees, admission charges, hire of facilities, catering);
(ii) grant aid from central government or quasi-public bodies such as the Tourist Boards, Sports Council, or Countryside Commission;
(iii) from the rates paid by local residents;
(iv) from central government Rate Support Grant.

(b) Private Sector Finance

The scale and type of private sector finance will depend on the scale of the project and the resources of the organisation planning the development. If it is a large organisation it may have sufficient capital reserves to finance new projects without borrowing, or can raise new capital through a share issue. If capital has to be borrowed there are two types of finance which relate to the timescale of the project. There is *fixed* capital to develop the land and buildings, plant and amenities, and the *short-term* capital to provide cash flow when the project is in its early stages of operation.

All tourism businesses, particularly small businesses will need short term finance for 1 to 3 years until the business becomes established. The most common source is overdraft facilities provided by the commercial clearing banks. An alternative source is using Hire Purchase Agreements to obtain fixed-term interest to meet the cost of plant and equipment.

Medium-term finance (4 to 8 years) is provided by the clearing banks, the Industrial and Commercial Finance Corporation (ICFC), the merchant banks, and the finance houses. Usually medium-term finance is at a variable rate of interest and this has the benefit of fixing the cost of money for the future and, where operating profits are high, paying for the capital loan out of net operating profit. This type of financing is particularly attractive if inflation increases and general interest rates rise.

Large scale projects involving say, capital investment of over £100,000 will require long-term finance (over 10 years) if the loan repayments are to be of a manageable size. These loans are mainly provided by insurance companies and building societies and some of the clearing banks.

Another source of finance is through sale and leaseback which can realise 100% of the valuation of a property. A case in point is the sea front development at Great Yarmouth, where a £5.7 million indoor leisure development was financed by a 25 year leaseback agreement between the Council and CIN Industrial Investments Ltd (a company wholly owned by the British Coal Pension Fund) for the sum of £4.5 million. The balance was funded by Lloyds Industrial Leasing Ltd.

Other sources of finance are through venture capital provided by the leading merchant banks or funds obtained through the government's Business Expansion Scheme.

Case Studies in Planning & Development

(a)   Tourism Development of Languedoc — Roussillon

This development was carried out between 1966 and 1980 by the French Government in close cooperation with local authorities and private interests. Its objective was the overall development of a 100 mile length of coastal strip in order to stimulate the stagnant local economy in the Languedoc-Roussillon area. The impetus behind the project was the growing pressure on the Cote d'Azur and the need to protect the undeveloped stretches of the Mediterranean coast from unplanned development. This region formed an almost uninterrupted stretch of large beaches often separated from the inland area by a series of lakes and salt marshes. Access was limited and roads were of poor quality.

The Languedoc-Roussillon development plans had three main objectives:

— To relieve pressure on the Cote D'Azur and meet the growing demand for mass tourism facilities on the Mediterranean coast.

— To raise the level of incomes in the region and by attracting both French and Foreign visitors help France's international balance of payments.

— To diversify a predominantly agricultural economy, provide employment for young people and stem the depopulation of the region.

In 1963 a government agency (Le Mission Interministerielle) was established to coordinate the activities of the State Ministries and to implement and supervise the development decisions. Joint public and private development companies were established and with the state providing the infrastructure needed for mass tourism, local development companies responsible for providing the ancilliary infrastructure, and the private sector responsible for construction and marketing.

Six new resort areas were developed (Fig 23 on page 108) with a total capacity of over 700,000 beds, capable of accommodating up to 3 million tourists a year. Each resort area has been zoned into areas for villas, apartments, hotels, holiday villages and camp-sites. The whole development has provided moorings for 20,000 boats and 80,000 new jobs. The construction of the new resorts involved the acquisition of 4,000 hectares of land at a cost (1970 prices) of £10 million. By 1980 the Development Commission, the mixed Development Boards, Local Authorities and the Private Sector had invested an estimated £600 million in the whole scheme.

A network of express motorways was created, linking the six new tourist resorts. Seven main marinas and thirteen smaller marinas were developed.

Figure 23: Resort Development in the Languedoc-Roussillon Region

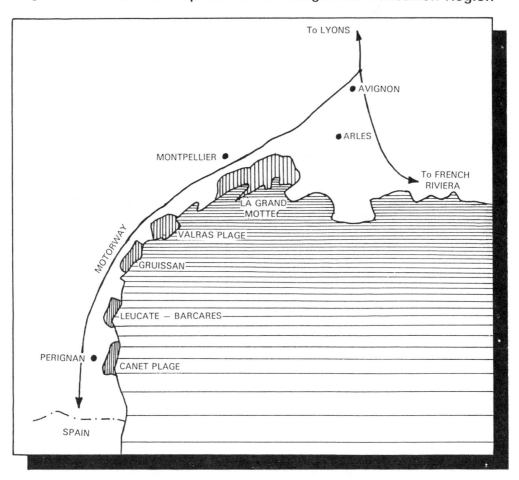

In addition a large-scale re-afforestation programme was implemented in what was a largely treeless region, and about 12,000 hectares has been planted.

Finance for the development companies was provided in the form of low interest loans from the Caisse des Depots and the Fund National d'Amenagement Foncier et d'Urbanisme. They developed improved the plots transferred to them by the State and then offered the improved land to private builders. The development costs were high, ranging from 50 francs to 2,000 francs per square metre. (*The Economist,* 1970).

This project achieved four main aims:

— it created a new tourist region, and provided important employment opportunities in a stagnant regional economy;

— it relieved pressure on the Cote d'Azur by opening up a 100 mile stretch of beaches;

— it controlled the type and location of development on a stretch of coast that had previously been developed in a piecemeal fashion;

— by a substantial programme of tree planting it reversed the extensive deforestation that had taken place since the nineteenth century.

One further by-product has been the rapid growth of new industry in the region attracted by the massive infrastructure developments and the attractive location.

(b)   Development of a Strategy for Hadrian's Wall

Hadrian's Wall is one of the finest archaeological and historic features in Britain and is unique in Western Europe. It is over 70 miles long and its chain of outer earthworks, milecastles and forts encompasses an area managed by three County Councils and six District Councils. Part of it lies within a National Park: two Regional Tourist Boards are responsible for promoting it and several national agencies have functions within this area. In addition there are many private interests concerned with the land on which the major remains are located.

From the early 1960s through to the 1970s there was a gradual but steady increase in the numbers of visitors to the Roman Wall particularly to the well known and accessible sites. This in turn led to problems of visitor pressure at specific locations along the Wall causing erosion of the monument and the main footpaths leading to it, and creating problems of congestion and access and lack of suitable services.

In 1974 the Countryside Commission appointed as consultants the Dartington Amenity Research Trust with the brief to 'appraise the existing and likely pressures on the Wall and its setting, give guidance on the broad planning strategy for their conservation, and to advise on traffic and visitor management and on interpretation and publicity related to the Wall'. In that year an officer working party was established, consisting of representatives of local authorities, the Countryside Commission, DoE Ancient Monuments branch, and the Regional and National Tourist Boards. Their brief was to consider the DART report and review comments on it, to prepare a strategy for the Wall and to seek its implementation.

In preparing the strategy it was clear that a wide range of interests had to be accommodated including landowners, farmers and local residents, local and County planning policies, archaeological and environmental issues, and the many other bodies with an interest in the land covered by the Wall.

Aims of the Strategy

The broad aims of the strategy were:

a)   to safeguard the splendid heritage of Roman monuments and all associated remains so that they are not lost or spoilt for future generations;

b)   to protect, and where possible enhance, the quality of landscape setting of the Wall sites;

c)   to encourage appropriate public visiting of the Wall area, with convenient access and high-quality experience and (for those who seek it) understanding of the Roman monuments and way of life.

d)   to ensure that local people derive the best possible benefits from tourism by way of income and employment, whilst ensuring that all appropriate steps are taken to minimise the adverse effects of tourism, particularly on agriculture.

Clearly, these aims may appear to conflict with one another. How can one safeguard the Roman heritage and protect the landscape quality of its setting whilst at the same time improving public access and encouraging the public to visit the Wall? With this in mind it was clear that any final strategy had to be realistic and practical if it was to be acceptable and capable of implementation.

Preparing a Strategy

The first step in the preparation of a strategy was to make a comprehensive assessment of all the relevant forts and earthworks and visible parts of the monument in the light of four criteria. These were:

— existing and protected number of visitors;

— environmental constraints;

— the appropriate timescale for proposed developments;

— land ownership.

(i)   Assessment of future visitor numbers to the Wall sites

Any plan for the Wall has to take account of growth or change in the numbers of visitors to the monument. As Figure 24 on page 111 shows, the numbers of visitors to the major sites grew rapidly between 1965 and 1973 when this upward trend was reversed after the sharp increase in petrol prices following the 1973 Arab-Israeli conflict. After 1973 numbers declined but have begun to increase again, albeit slowly, in the 1980s. The Northumberland Structure Plan assumes a general growth in the numbers of visitors to the countryside in the order of 2 to 3 per cent per year, and other indicators suggest that this may be an underestimate. However, even with a growth rate of two to three per cent per year this would bring back visitor numbers at Chesters and Vindolanda to previous peak levels by the early 1990s. Other factors that may influence this growth are the development of Keilder Water as a major tourist attraction and the designation of the North Pennines as an area of outstanding natural beauty. In addition to forecasts in the long-term growth in visitor numbers an assessment was made of the potential peak usage at the 9 major sites along the Wall, taking into account development proposals, development of visitor services and increased car parking (Table 23 on page 112).

(ii)   Environmental constraints

These estimates were then related to the ability of the major sites to accommodate visitors. Four environmental criteria were used to determine the acceptable number of visitors:

110

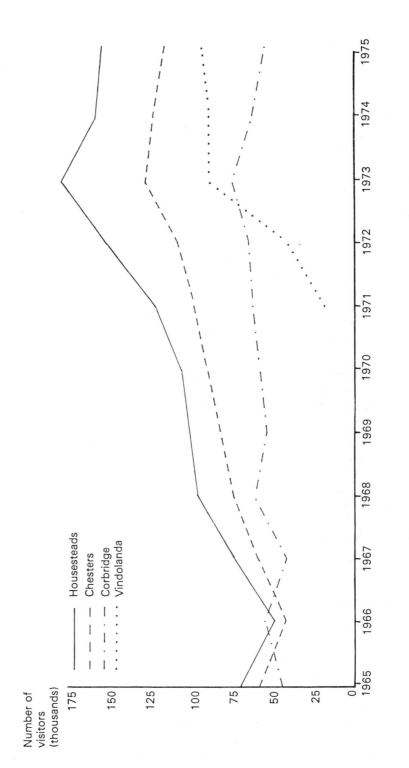

Figure 24: Growth in Tourists to the Roman Wall

Annual totals of visitors to four major sites 1965 to 1975

Number of
visitors
(thousands)

Housesteads
Chesters
Corbridge
Vindolanda

Source: *Countryside Commission: (Dart Report)*

Table 23:
Forecasts of Peak Capacity at Main Sites on Roman Wall

Site	Annual No. Of Visitors	Forecast Peak Capacity At Any One Time
Birdoswald	NA	250—400
Carvoran	NA	480
Vindolanda	80,000	600—650
Housesteads	113,000	450
Carrowbrough	NA	40
Chesters	101,000	1,000
Corbridge	28,000	1,200
Rudchester	NA	200
South Shields	40,000	450

Source: A Strategy for Hadrians Wall. *Countryside Commission*1984

a)   the capacity of the landscape in the Wall corridor to absorb the infrastructure which visitors need, e.g. car parks, access roads, toilet blocks, picnic sites;

b)   the effect of visitor pressures on farming and the capacity of existing and proposed footpaths, including that along the Wall and other factors;

c)   the implications for nature conservation (a subject of particular concern in the consultation exercise);

d)   the protection of the archaeological fabric itself particularly from the effects of increased visiting.

The Strategy for Major Sites

After reviewing the Dartington Amenity Research Trust's recommendations for each site and making a site-by-site assessment on the lines set out above, four categories of site were identified.

(i)   Sites where no development is envisaged

These are sites which *either* are not of strategic importance or where there are particular considerations which would restrict development in the foreseeable future. There are 3 such sites: Great Chesters, Housesteads and Carrawbrough (Brocolitia). At Great Chesters visitor numbers are small and there is a well established working farm. At Housesteads the site already receives over 100,000 visitors a year and it was felt that any major increase in visitor numbers would lead to unacceptable wear and tear on the monument and the access routes to it, and would greatly diminish the quality of the visitor's experience. At Carrawbrough (Brocolitia) visitors are attracted because of the Mithraic temple which has been excavated. The present site capacity is low and the existing car park is already intrusive. Any further car parking provision should be discouraged.

(ii) *Sites where limited development would be acceptable*

These are sites where limited improvements in car parking, access and visitor facilities could occur, but which would not be able to absorb large-scale developments. There are 2 sites, Birdoswold and Vindolanda. Birdoswold is the most westerly fort in the central section of the Wall and is in a very fine landscape setting. The difficulties of access via narrow roads from Gilsland or Lanercost, and the impact of any large car parks on the site are major constraints. However, because of the great archaeological potential of the site, the willingness of the Department of the Environment to support some excavation, its location well to the West of the central section, and its acquisition by Cumbria County Council, it was felt that limited development should be a priority. Vindolanda is a major civilian settlement excavated in the 1970s, with a new museum. It currently receives around 80,000 visitors a year. However, road access is difficult and the existing car and coach parks are very obtrusive and it will be some time before planting around them provides an effective screen. At peak times in the visitor season overcrowding and congestion are very evident.

(iii) *Sites with major development potential*

These are sites that have the space to accommodate increased visitor numbers and facilities without damaging the monument or the landscape setting, where the intrinsic interest is very great, and where existing accessibility is good. There are 4 such sites — Carvoran, Chesters, Corbridge and South Shields.

(iv) *Sites with long-term potential*

These are sites with a high intrinsic interest but because of existing circumstances there is no opportunity for development in the immediate future. However, they were considered to have important potential for development in the long-term. There are 5 sites Maryport, Portgate, Halton-Chesters, Rudchester and Wallsend.

Since Victorian times the Roman Wall has been recognised as a major archaeological monument and tourist attraction. By the 1970s wear and tear caused soil erosion and in parts the foundations of the Wall itself began to erode as the soil was washed away. Visitors found the main sites crowded at peak times, there was a lack of visitor services and interpretive facilities were limited. The DART report highlighted these problems but it was clear that no single organisation could provide a solution because the Wall extends over such a large area, with a great number of different landowners and cuts across several local authority boundaries. For the first time 32 public and private organisations came together to prepare a single policy framework for decisions affecting the whole length of the Wall.

(c) Portsmouth Harbour Tourism Development Action Programme

This programme was one of over 14 tourism development action programmes initiated by the English Tourist Board during the 1980s. It was a joint venture undertaken on a partnership basis by Portsmouth City Council, Gosport Borough

Council, the English Tourist Board, Hampshire County Council and the Southern Tourist Board between 1985 and 1989. The aim of the TDAP was to stimulate and develop tourism in Portsmouth and Gosport. The primary focus of this action programme was the immediate surroundings of Portsmouth Harbour although it did include initiatives elsewhere in Portsmouth and Gosport. It was designed to complement and strengthen existing tourism development initiatives such as the Portsmouth Naval Heritage Project and the Hampshire Defence Heritage Project and other schemes undertaken by both the public and private sector. The overall objective was to use tourism as a central factor in enhancing the economic prospect for the area by stimulating economic development and creating new jobs. This latter point was particularly important with local unemployment levels at over 12%. An Economic Impact Study commissioned in 1985 estimated that in Portsmouth 10,000 jobs in accommodation, catering, transport, retailing and related services were directly supported by tourism.

The plan area (Figure 22) contains a wide range of attractions and underlines the potential for the harbour area to attract more tourists and more repeat visits. The key to the action programme was the Portsmouth Naval Heritage Project which formed part of the Portsmouth Naval Base. It contains:

— the Mary Rose Ship Hall and Exhibition. This is a Tudor Warship built in 1510 sunk in 1545 and recovered (with many relics of the period) in 1982.

— HMS Victory, Admiral Lord Nelson's flagship at the Battle of Trafalgar which has been on display since 1922.

— HMS Warrior, built in 1860 as the first British iron-hulled warship, fully restored and returned to the harbour in 1988.

— Royal Naval Museum. This has artifacts and memorabilia from over 500 years of naval history.

The town also contains numerous other tourist attractions including the D-Day Museum, the Submarine Museum, Gosport, Southsea Castle, Dicken's Birthplace Museum as well as traditional seaside resort facilities.

There were several factors which suggested that Portsmouth was a good choice for a TDAP. These included:

— the unique nature of the Maritime Heritage project and its appeal to both domestic and overseas tourists.

— a strong marketing and development team already in place.

— accessibility to an extensive hinterland and the existence of strong links with France through a ferry route.

— local authorities favourably disposed towards tourism and a commitment to local authority investment in the tourism infrastructure.

However, there were existing weaknesses. The area in 1985 suffered badly from a shortage of modern good quality hotel accommodation and had limited self-catering facilities. City centre shopping facilities were poor. The area had no purpose-built Conference or Exhibition facilities. On-site information and interpretative facilities were very limited. Signposting was poor both in the city and in the surrounding area. Car and coach parking were inadequate especially in the Naval dockyard area.

Portsmouth had a poor image as a tourist destination. Many saw it simply as a dockyard city and people confused it with Plymouth, unaware of its exact location.

Key Tourism Issues in the TDAP

The Tourism Development Action Programme focussed on 6 key issues:

(1) Raising the tourism profile
(ii) Identifying and developing the potential of the Heritage Attractions
(iii) Improving the visitor's experience of the area
(iv) Developing other attractions, events and activities
(v) Increasing the amount and improving the quality of the areas's accommodation both serviced and self-catering
(vi) Conducting specific marketing campaigns at the major sectors of tourist demand.

Within the plan area tourism priority areas were identified where priority was given to improving the facilities and environment for tourism through planning policies and development programmes. The scheme brought together three local authorities, the English Tourist Board and the Southern Tourist Board.

Public Sector involvement was mainly designed to provide a climate where tourism developments would be encouraged to take place provided they met the broad aims of the development programme. The different levels of investment between the public and private sector highlight this point. At the initiation of the TDAP the public sector had allocated £50,000 to £60,000 whereas private sector tourism related development in Portsmouth amounted to over £50 million. (Portsmouth Harbour TDAP report Appendix 2).

ASSIGNMENTS

1. You are a farmer with 400 acres of good quality farmland on the South Devon coast. 10 acres are partly wooded, gently sloping land that you wish to develop as a small holiday village. The site is served by a 'B' road. Put together a proposal setting out:

    a) the main aims of the project including the market to be served and the level of use envisaged;

    b) the proposed sources of financing and phasing of expenditure;

    c) a case to the local planning authority setting out why this site should be developed for tourism.

2. You are a director of a regional Tourist Board. Prepare a paper setting out your regional plan for tourism development over the next 5 years. In this paper you should consider existing provision of facilities, distribution of resources, existing and planned infrastructure and proposals for new tourism developments over the plan period.

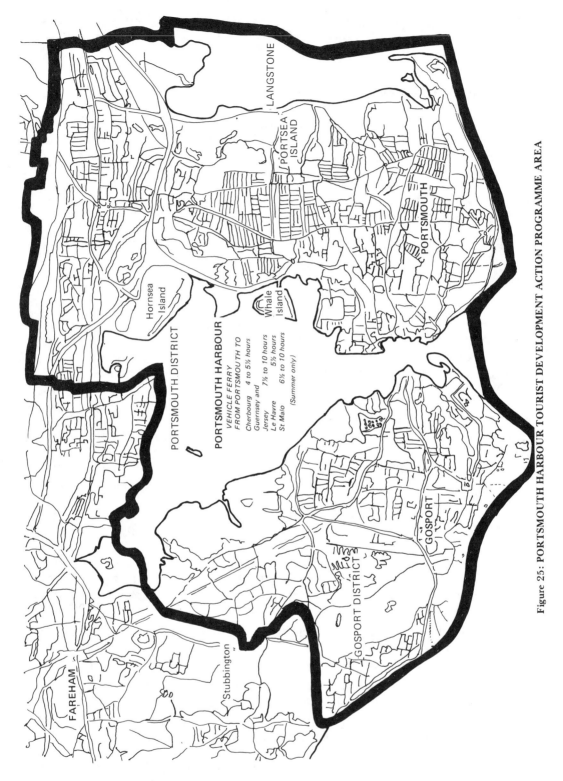

LANGSTONE

PORTSEA ISLAND

PORTSMOUTH

Hornsea Island

Whale Island

PORTSMOUTH DISTRICT

PORTSMOUTH HARBOUR

*VEHICLE FERRY
FROM PORTSMOUTH TO*

Cherbourg   4 to 5½ hours
Guernsey and
Jersey   7½ to 10 hours
Le Havre   5¾ hours
St Malo   6½ to 10 hours

(Summer only)

GOSPORT

GOSPORT DISTRICT

FAREHAM

Stubbington

Figure 25: PORTSMOUTH HARBOUR TOURIST DEVELOPMENT ACTION PROGRAMME AREA

Chapter 10

Tourism Marketing

Learning Objectives: After reading this chapter you should have a clear understanding of:

— the difference between selling and marketing;

— identifying the tourist product;

— the elements of market research;

— market segmentation;

— advertising, publicity and promotion as marketing tools;

— the main elements of a marketing plan.

Introduction

Marketing covers a wide range of activities including promoting, selling and developing a product. Marketing is a process which involves persuading a potential buyer that a particular product or service is the most suitable for his or her needs. This is relatively straightforward if the product is a motor car or detergent. It is less so if the product is a tourist product. The demand for the tourism product is entirely discretionary.

It is not essential and is influenced by people's tastes, perceptions and preferences and other intangible factors. The tourism product is often seasonal and if 'unsold' by a particular date it is lost. Unlike a manufactured article which can be reduced in price or sold at a later date, an airline seat or hotel bedroom has to be sold by a set date otherwise it has no value/earning potential. In order to overcome these problems a tourism marketing plan needs to be developed which includes the following stages:

— identifying the existing tourism product;

— undertaking market research to identify the psychology of the tourist, the market segments, the strengths and weaknesses of the tourism product;

— modifying the tourism product in response to the market research (product strategy);

— identifying the marketing mix;

— promotion, including advertising and publicity;

— selling the tourism product;

— analysing the results of the marketing strategy and modifying it if necessary.

Each of these elements may be thought of as tourism marketing — but in isolation they are not. Together they make up marketing. It is a cyclical process, with periodic reviews of the product-market mix and the promotional strategy, in order to measure their effectiveness and to decide whether new strategies are needed.

117

The Tourist Product

In Chapter 3 the tourism product is defined as the resort or historic town, the beaches, scenery, mountains, historic sites, theme parks, museums and other tourist attractions, as well as the accommodation stock. The difference between this and almost any other product is that the consumer (i.e. the market for the product) travels to the place of production and consumes the product on the spot. So tourism marketing must take account of the psychology of the traveller as well as the consumer.

The travel element of the tourism product may simply be a means of getting from home to resort as quickly and as cheaply as possible. Or, it may be an end in itself as with cruising, or the Orient Express, where the journey *is* the product. Again a distinction must be made between discretionary travel (tourist travel) and non-discretionary travel (business travel). The marketing approach is quite different in each case.

A less tangible element of the tourism product, but in many ways the most important, is the quality of service provided to the tourist (the consumer). It is not enough to identify who the customers are and what their needs are. It is important to remember that customer satisfaction depends on the standards of quality and service meeting the expectations of customers. If a charter flight is cancelled or a hotel room is over-booked it can affect the whole holiday experience. Similarly, poor service cannot be retrieved and can lead to adverse publicity and a decline in trade. An emphasis on quality control and staff training in customer relations, are essential elements of a good tourism product.

Seasonality may be a key influence on the tourism product. Sales may be concentrated into four or five months, and the level of sales during that period must be sufficient to make the business financially viable.

Good marketing can help to extend the season, identify new client groups, develop new pricing strategies, and improve the profitability of a tourism business.

As the tourist industry has developed, certain elements such as international hotels or major airlines have evolved a broadly similar product. One jumbo jet is very similar to another regardless of the logo; a 4-star hotel should have similar facilities regardless of its location. This raises the question of how do companies offering a very similar product succeed in persuading the public to choose them in preference to their competitors? The answer is found in their marketing strategy. In order to develop a marketing strategy you need to know as much as possible about the market. In order to obtain this information it is necessary to undertake market research. The following section outlines the principles and practice of market research.

Market Research

This should provide answers to the following questions:

— what is the total size of the tourist market?
— who are the existing customers?
— where are they from?
— what are the existing customers seeking?

— what level of pricing (in relation to facilities), will the customers accept?
— what are the past and existing trends in the tourist market?
— what factors influence these trends?
— who are the potential future customers?
— what are the strengths and weaknesses of the product compared with competitors?

Market research uses two types of data — primary and secondary.

Primary Data can be obtained from two sources, from in-house data and from field surveys. *In-house data* can provide information about the performance of the business, measured by daily, weekly, monthly figures on:

— occupancy rates
— visitor spending
— sources of business
— profit margins
— revenue costs

This can be analysed for an individual business or group of businesses or a region — if the data is available.

Field surveys

These can take several forms, but the most frequent means of collect ing primary data is by using questionnaires. These can be either self completed or fill-ed in by trained researchers during personal interviews. Self completed questionnaires are commonly used by hotels and airlines but they suffer from two main drawbacks which seriously limit their value for market research. They allow no control over the 'sample' of tourists completing and returning the questionnaires. It is not a representative sample and often consists of people who were dissatisfied with some aspect of the facility/service provided.

In carrying out field surveys the most valuable results are generally obtained by taking a random sample and using a trained interviewer to complete a structured questionnaire during personal interviews. A *random* sample assumes that it is un-biased and representative of the population being studied. Using random number tables and names drawn from the Electoral Register it is possible to produce a general random sample. However, in doing field surveys with interviews at airports or harbours or hotels, it is more difficult to produce a genuine random sample, and it may be more practical to produce *a stratified sample* where the data and the sample are related to particular groups weighted according to the proportion in each group as part of the total population.

The questionnaire generally provides two types of data. First there is the demographic and socio-economic profile of the tourist. That is, the age, family composition, income, occupation and place of residence of the tourist, and their spending patterns on holiday. The second set of data relate to the opinions, perceptions and motivations of the tourist — in relation to a particular tourist product and/or competing tourist products. The way in which these more subjective questions are put and the order in which they are put is a critical aspect of questionnaire design.

119

Secondary-Data can be obtained by undertaking Desk Research using census returns, company reports, local, regional, national or international tourist surveys, general household surveys, studies of leisure trends, and reports from trade associations and professional bodies. This can provide information on tourism trends and changing public preferences over time. In Britain the National and Regional Tourist Boards regularly publish a wide range of statistics on tourism trends.

In the United States the US Travel Data Centre based in Washington DC publishes frequent reports on many aspects of travel and tourism. Most of this information is readily available, either in public libraries or at a relatively low cost.

The Marketing Mix

Having undertaken the market research, using either desk surveys, or field surveys or a combination of both, the resort or tourist company should have acquired a mass of information about the elements of their tourist product that attract or detract tourists, the preferences and attitudes of the tourist, and an extensive profile of the different types of tourist that together make up the 'market'. One of the first questions requiring an answer is 'What factors influence the tourist to buy my product?' or 'How did he hear of my product?' These and related questions enable businesses within the tourist industry to design or modify a product that will improve their competitiveness and ultimately their profitability. The consumer, in this case, the tourist, is rarely buying a single product. He or she is buying a set of 'products' that appeal to him or her and the choice of product may be influenced by income, education, age and life-style. The preference may be for exclusive, exotic, cultural tours or low cost self-catering beach holidays with guaranteed sunshine. Between the high cost low volume trade and the low cost mass market there are a wide range of possible products. Ideally a tourist region, or resort or individual business aims to develop a range of tourism products that will appeal to the widest possible market. This is known as the *product mix*. So a resort will offer a wide range of types of accommodation and a variety of forms of entertainment. Special pricing packages for hotels or airlines within a range of prices/fares are also examples of product mix.

After the market research is complete, a profile of the tourist can be constructed and the product can be improved or modified to make it more competitive in the marketplace. The next step must be to examine the ways in which the consumer is made aware of the product. Unless and until the customer knows of the existence of a product he or she will not be able to consider buying it. The product is made known to the tourist by a method known as the *communications mix*. This is done in a variety of ways including:

— direct marketing (mailshots, telephone canvassing, etc.);
— media displays (TV ads, newspapers, magazines etc.);
— special events/promotions;
— exhibitions, (trade shows, displays etc.).

The tourism 'product' is often a combination of elements including transport, accommodation, amenities and entertainments. The way in which these products are sold to the consumer is known as the *distribution mix*. This mix can include inclusive tours bought through travel agents, or direct sell holidays or special promotions carried out by the airlines or selected hotels. There are a great variety of possible distribution channels, and the aim of a marketing strategy should be to use these as cost-effectively as possible, so as to reach the greatest possible number of potential tourists. Every tourist business, resort, or region is in competition with other tourist destinations, and it is the firm or organisation that keeps its distribution costs (and hence its product costs) down that will be the most competitive. Price/cost is not the only criterion, although it is important. The product must be attractive and marketed in an effective way if tourists are to be persuaded to buy it.

Product Life Cycle

If the sales of the product are plotted on a graph, a successful product — in this case a hotel resort or airline — will show an upward curve on the sales chart. This will continue until the market is saturated and the number of consumers (tourists) will either remain static or even decline, showing a downward curve (Figure 25 on page 122). This cycle, from the introduction of a product through to its demise or saturation is known as the *product life* and this may be measured in years or decades. The life of the product can be extended in two principal ways:

(i)   by finding new markets for the product; or
(ii) by redeveloping the product to meet changing tastes and preferences.

Market Segmentation

This is a term for the process where companies or organisations will identify particular groups within the population who are potential buyers for the tourist product, and the marketing strategy will target these market segments. Market research should help to identify these target markets. These segments are made of four broad groups:

(i)   the youth market;
(ii)   the family market;
(iii) the senior citizen market;
(iv)   the special interest market.

The tourist market can also be grouped by region, with a concentration of marketing effort on the main tourist generating regions. The main markets are those countries or regions who provide say over 30% of the main tourist flows. The pricing policies, promotional campaigns and advertising will focus on these areas. Then there are the secondary markets who provide some tourists to a particular destination but who have considerable potential traffic which is at present going to other destinations. Finally there are targets of opportunity which are new, rapidly growing economies who are historically of little significance as generators of tourists, but these emerging markets may be attracted to existing tourist destinations.

Figure 26 : The Product Life Cycle

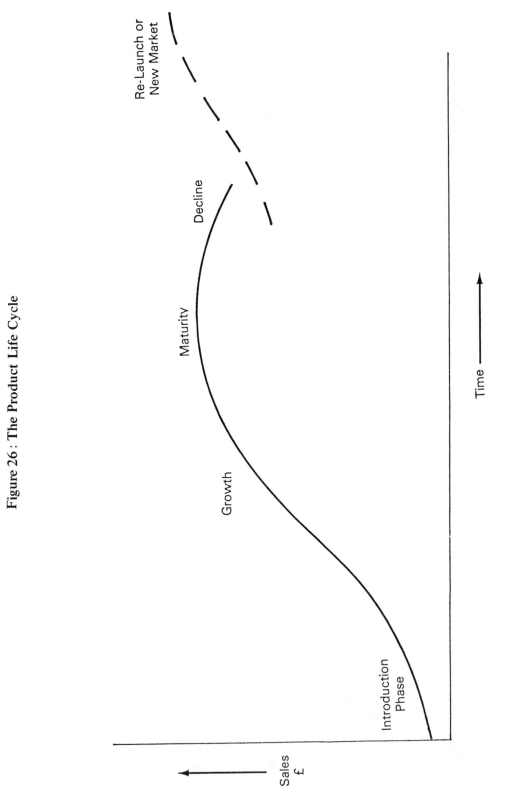

Pricing Policy

This is a further crucial element in any marketing strategy. In order to arrive at the most effective price the following information is needed:

(i) the cost of producing the product;

(ii) the planned volume of sales;

(iii) the prices charged by competitors;

(iv) other external factors such as interest rates, fuel surcharges etc.

(v) consumer's views on prices;

(vi) the level of investment required to produce the target sale to achieve a marginal rate of return on that investment.

A number of pricing policies may be used, varying according to the nature of the tourism product and the forecasted life cycle of that product. Where a tourist business or region is trying to break into an established market a policy of lowering prices and hence profit margins may be introduced, with the longer term aim of gradually increasing prices once a market share has been established. This is known as *penetration pricing*.

Promotional pricing may be used to attract customers for a new product or to revive flagging sales of an old product. Here a lower price than normal would be introduced.

Where there is high initial investment and an early recovery of this is needed the organisation may introduce high prices and then progressively lower them as competition increases. This is known as *skim pricing*.

Pricing policy can also be used as a planning tool, if for example, a region, resort or hotel wishes to concentrate on an up-market clientele it may deliberately choose to impose high prices as a means of controlling the influx of tourists.

Selling the Product

Having done the market research, developed a product, identified market segments, established a pricing policy and made customers aware of the product, it must be sold to them. Making a sale is the final part of the communications mix. If the seller is a retail travel agent he or she has to identify the client's needs and suggest the best destination for that tourist. If it is an inclusive tour does it provide the right kind of accommodation, at the right price and in the right location? Are the travel arrangements satisfactory? If the seller is promoting/selling a particular product they need to convince the particular customer that the product will meet their needs and at a price they can afford. They need to know the product in detail and the strengths and weaknesses of competing products. Selling the benefits of a particular product is an important part of the sale. As soon as the seller is aware that the customer is willing to buy they should seek to close the sale and seek to ask for the business.

Preparing a Marketing Strategy

The first step in preparing a marketing strategy is to establish the main goals and objectives of the firm or organisation. In the case of tourism marketing there is generally a combination of:

(i)   increasing the market share of the product;

(ii)   increasing the profits from tourist spending;

(iii) developing new tourist markets;

(iv) reviving declining tourist products.

These are general long-term objectives and there is often a difference in objectives between those of the national or regional tourist organisation and the individual business who is usually selling a specific product to a specific segment of the market. Small tourism businesses often do not have a marketing plan and usually have not undertaken any market research. These are the most vulnerable element in the tourism industry.

There is an element of risk in any marketing strategy in that expenditure has to take place on developing a tourist product and marketing that product *before* the business or organisation is in a position to measure the success of the strategy. Forecasting the outcome of particular strategies is an important element in market research and can be used to predict not only the probability of success of a strategy, but also the degree of risk involved.

There are six main stages in preparing a marketing strategy. These are:

(i)   *identify the target market segments.* This relates to the age and socio-economic profile and region of origin of consumers (tourists) and decisions on whether a high volume mass market or low volume high spending exclusive market is desired.

(ii)   *identify the consumer's profile for these market segments.* Market research among the target population can identify the preferences of the target market and those aspects of the product mix which have most appeal.

(iii) *identify the key factors which influence the segment's decision to buy a holiday.* Is it price? Is it conditioned by the image of the product? Is it the availability of distribution channels? Is it influenced by socio-political factors?

(iv) *establish the pricing policy.* This has already been discussed, but it is important in relation to whether the strategy is aimed at new markets, fighting off competition from other tourist regions, optimising income year-round or changing the image of the product.

(v)   *relate the marketing mix to the factors which most influence the client's decision-buying process.* This may involve a review of the product mix, the distribution mix and the communications mix in the light of factors that persuade the consumer to buy a particular tourist product. If he or she knows little about the product there is clearly a case for looking at the effectiveness of the communications mix.

(vi) *identify the main groups of clients.* There are usually two or three groups of client. In the first stage of the distribution mix there are the retailers (travel agents) and the wholesalers and general tour operators. They will require particular discounts or special offers in order to promote and sell the product. In the second group there are the tourists themselves, and the marketing strategy must cater for them also. Finally there are the business travellers who are influenced by differential pricing but more concerned with factors such as reliability, comfort, frequency of service and quality of service.

Measuring the Performance of a Marketing Strategy

In any marketing strategy it is necessary to build in a control and evaluation mechanism so that the oganisation can measure the success of its policies and if need be change them in the light of new information. One effective method is to keep weekly and monthly sales (and booking) figures and plot them on a graph to show:

(i)   weekly and monthly sales compared to previous years;

(ii) cumulative sales to date showing performance over the year up to the present (perhaps against target figures);

(iii) deviations from a regression line which shows long-term trends.

If these sets of indices are plotted the graph will show a Z shape (Figure 26 on page 126). This provides a clear picture of this year's performance compared to last year when measured by monthly sales and cumulative sales, and should show that the long-term trend is up or static or in decline. Clearly this technique is readily applicable to an individual business and less so to a tourist resort or region as a whole, *unless* there are detailed statistics available on tourist numbers and spending over a period of years.

An alternative method is to tabulate the weekly/monthly budget forecast of sales and the actual sales for the same period, and to measure the shortfalls or surpluses that occur, and if necessary modify the marketing strategy. *Analysis of variance* is a commonly used statistical method, and for more detailed consideration of this see Gregory (1971).

The tourist industry is continuing to grow as new firms, new destinations, new kinds of tourist product and new markets are developed.

For example, Chapter 6 discussed the impact of deregulation of coach and air transport and forecast changes in aircraft technology in the 1990s. Both of these developments are already having a significant impact on the tourism industry. Chapter 13 includes references to time-share, theme parks and inner city tourism. All the evidence points to the dynamic and fast-changing nature of travel and tourism and underlines the need for effective marketing. This growth in activity brings with it increasing competition as businesses seek a greater market share. It is clear that any tourist business — from the largest company or national tourist office to the small family business — must develop a marketing strategy if it is to survive and prosper.

Any marketing plan should include the following elements. In developing a tourism product it should be evaluated for its:

Strengths (i.e. how does it compare over other similar products?)

Weaknesses (i.e. where is it deficient compared to competing products?)

Opportunities (i.e. what new markets or market segments exist for this product?)

Threats (Who are the main competitors and what are they doing in the marketplace?)

125

Figure 27: A Typical 'Z' Graph

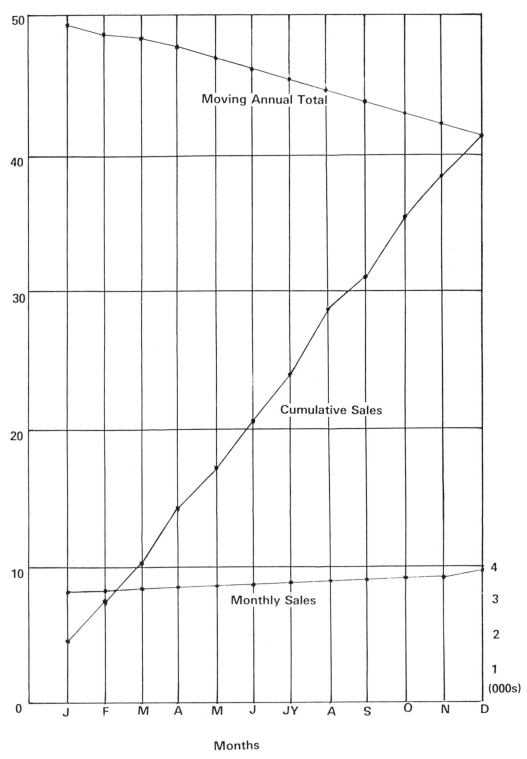

Months

In addition to the acronym SWOT which sums up the evaluation process, the business of marketing revolves around four P's:

Product   This can be summed up as the scenic, climatic, cultural, historic features that attract tourists; the range of services to transport them to and from their destination, and the facilities to accommodate them during their stay here.

Price   This is of crucial importance in marketing tourism because of the high level of competition between many tourist products. Pricing may be used as a marketing tool, to establish a niche in an existing market, to fight of competition to retain market share, or to present an image of exclusiveness. Pricing policy is usually not static and can vary according to the nature of the tourist product.

Place   This is not only the resort or tourist attraction, it means all the locations where the potential tourist can buy the tourist product. Thus high street retail travel agents and direct sell tour operators who are selling tourist products are a key factor in the marketing process. Tourist Information Centres and other points of sale are also included under 'Place'.

Promotion   This includes advertising, production of brochures, public relations, sales promotion and is the most recognisable of the four P's. It is often taken to be synonymous with marketing but is only *part* of the marketing process.

Each of these P's has a key role to play in evolving a marketing strategy. However, to be successful they must be seen as part of an overall decision-making process which aims to match the needs and wishes of market segments with particular tourist products, to sell the product as effectively as possible and to maintain or increase market share for the firm or organisation concerned.

Conclusions

The tourist industry is continuing to grow as new firms, new destinations and new markets are developed.

The growth of de-regulation of transport (see Chapter 6) and the emergence of new tourist generating countries underline the continual need for effective marketing. This growth in activity brings with it increasing competition as businesses seek a greater market share. It is clear that any organisation in the tourist industry, from the National Tourist Organisation or the multi-national company to the small tourist business, should have a marketing strategy if it is to prosper.

ASSIGNMENTS

1. You are a marketing consultant charged with preparing a marketing plan for a new company seeking to develop exclusive package holidays to selected long-haul exotic destinations. Prepare a proposal setting out your choice of destinations and market segments. Identify the strengths and weaknesses of existing competitiors.

2. You are the owner/manager of a large hotel in a downtown location in a major resort. Your room occupancy is below average and you have a suite of large rooms on the ground floor that are greatly under-used. Suggest how you might develop a marketing plan to increase your occupancy levels and the usage of your ground floor rooms.

Chapter 11

Tourism Impact Studies
1: The Economic Impact of Tourism

Learning Objectives: After reading this chapter you should understand:

— the way in which tourism affects the economy of a
   town or region;
— the 'multiplier effect';
— the main methods of measuring economic impacts
   of tourism;
— the impact of tourism on the national economy.

Introduction

Tourism as a phenomenon has two kinds of impact. In the first place tourists bring in income to a region through their spending on goods and services there. Secondly, wherever it occurs, tourism has an impact on the environment both through the infrastructure that is part of the tourism development process, and the impact of the tourists themselves on the culture and society of the tourist region. This chapter and the following one will look in detail at these different kinds of impact and in particular consider:

— What is the nature of these impacts?
— How can we measure them?
— What are the consequences of these impacts?
— What are the implications for future planning and develop
   ment of tourism?

This chapter attempts to examine the economic impact of tourism and looks at ways of measuring this.

Tourist Expenditure

Tourist spending is made up of several components related to the different stages in the holiday package. If it is an inclusive tour the tourist will have paid for the holiday in his home country and the bulk of this money will remain with the operator and retailer and carrier. A proportion will go to the hotel in the tourist regions.

The main spending in the tourist region will therefore tend to be on:

— Meals and drinks out;
— Entertainment;
— Car hire or travel in the region;
— Gifts and souvenirs.

However, measurement of economic impacts is more complex than this, in that income comes not just from visitor spending, but also from wages and salaries of those working in the tourist industry, profits that tourist businesses make, and interest on capital borrowed to develop tourist projects.

METHODS OF MEASURING THE IMPACT OF TOURISM ON THE ECONOMY

1. On Regional and Local Economies

The concept of measuring the economic benefits on regional economies of particular activities by means of particular models is not new, and appears in books and articles on regional economic analysis going back over the past 40 years. However, the application of these models to tourism as an economic activity is much more recent. For a general introduction to methods of regional economic analysis, two useful references are W Isard — *Methods of Regional Analysis* (1970) and H Richardson — *Elements of Regional Economics* (1970).

There are three main methods generally used and these vary in their applicability and effectiveness.

Table 24:
A Transactions Matrix

Producing Industry	Consuming Industry					
	Sector 1	Sector 2	Sector 3	Sector 4	Final Demand	Total Output
Primary	20	130	20	10	20	200
Manufacturing	80	50	70	150	50	400
Services	30	10	10	10	180	240
Other	30	20	100	100	200	450
Value Added	40	190	40	180		
Total Input	200	400	240	450		

There are three main methods generally used and these vary in their applicability and effectiveness.

These are:

— the economic base method;
— input-output analysis;
— the multiplier method;

(a) The Economic Base Method

This method divides the economic activities of a region into those that are *basic* and *non-basic*. The *basic* activities are considered to be those exported to other regions and which bring income and generate jobs in the area in which they are based. The *non-basic* sector depends on and services the basic sector and the size of the *non-basic* sector is dependent on the level of economic activity in the *basic* sector.

It is therefore a very simple model, which is based on 3 assumptions:

— all economic activity is either basic or non-basic;
— economic performance can be measured by the performance of the basic sector;
— there is a constant relationship between the size of the basic sector and the size of the non-basic sector.

If the number of jobs provided by the basic and non-basic activities can be identified, then it is possible to establish the ratio between them and to calculate the number of new jobs created in the non-basic category, following a growth in exports (in this case tourism).

However, this method is limited in its application not least because it is difficult to identify all the basic and non-basic activities. It overlooks the fact the firms may have activities that are both basic and non-basic, and that there may be linkages between basic and non-basic operations. Also it is questionable whether the non-basic sector *is* entirely dependent on the basic sector and whether the ratio between the two sectors remains constant. In the case of tourist activity, as a region grows, a proportion of the domestic population may consume the local tourist product and later the basic/non-basic ratio.

(b) Input-Output Analysis

This is based on the concept that the economy of a region (or place) can be divided into producing sectors and consuming sectors. Input-output analysis attempts to model the inter-relationships between the producing and consuming sectors of the economy.

A detailed account of the methodology of input-output analysis is provided in Isard (1970), but the broad concept is developed by producing a matrix of transactions between the producing and consuming sectors. As Table 24. on page 130 shows, the producing sector forms the rows on the vertical axis and the consuming sector the columns on the horizontal axis. It is possible by using this matrix to discover how much each industry purchases from other industries and how much of the output of each economic activity is allocated to other industries in the region. Although Table 24 shows three main sectors, these could be disaggregated into individual industries within each sector to produce a much more detailed and complex transactions matrix.

The main problems associated with applying this method to regional economic analysis generally, and to the tourism industry in particular, are that it is dependent on identifying the representative set of industries and calculating constant coefficients to explain the transactions between them. It is also dependent on having available extensive data sets on regional income and employment levels in a sufficiently disaggregated form to identify particular facets of the tourist industry and at a local or regional level. In many tourist regions the economic theory is in advance of the data needed to apply it.

(c) The Multiplier Method

The concept of a *multiplier* has been used by economists since the 1930s at least, but it was Keynes who provided a much more precise application of this approach.

The *multiplier concept* is based on the premise that initial spending within a region will inject additional cash into the flow of income in the regional economy, and thus increase the regional income. The size of the income multiplier is based on the proportion of the additional income that is spent *within* the region to be received as income by other businesses who in turn will spend a proportion of this income within this region and so on. The more that the intitial injection of cash is re-spent within the region, the greater will be the rise in total income.

However, not all this income will be spent, or if spent remain within the region. There will be 'leakages', for example savings or spending on goods and sevices from other regions with each successive iteration there will be a certain amount of 'leakage' out of the system and the amount of additional income generated will decline.

The application of the multiplier method to estimates of the regional economic benefits of tourism was developed during the 1970s by B H Archer (1973), D R Vaughan (1977) and others. These studies identified visitor spending by carrying out extensive on-site questionnaire surveys together with information from particular local businesses that were thought to be either representative of the local tourist industry or related to/dependent on the local tourist industry.

These surveys generally attempted to identify three separate sets of data on:

— *direct spending,* that is expenditure of visitors on services/facilities provided by hotels, restaurants, shops and other local businesses/facilities;

— *generated spending,* which is indirect spending resulting from the further purchase of goods and services by the tourist businesses in which the visitors have spent their money;

— *additional spending* by local residents of the income they have earned, directly or indirectly from visitor spending.

For each type of visitor a profile was prepared showing the impact of spending and the successive stages that this income progressed through as it circulated in the local economy. For example if a family spend £500 in a local hotel, the hotel will in turn use this income to pay for the wages and salaries of staff, buying food and supplies, paying laundry bills and banking the profit. Some of these purchases or services will be provided by local businesses who will in turn use this income to pay wages, meet other costs and keep as profit the residue. Table 18 on page 143 shows a hypothetical example and shows that by using the multiplier method in this way, for every £500 spent by a visitor £145 is generated as additional income. So in this case the multiplier would be 0.29.

In addition to direct visitor spending in hotels and local facilities such studies have attempted to survey the main business activities related to tourism in order to produce a coefficient which will reflect the additional income generated. After both types of survey have been completed, the end result is a composite multiplier as an index of all three types of income generated.

The approach developed by Archer (1973) and others is based on a concept that is in itself simple, but which requires extremely complex data collection and analysis to apply in practice. For multiplier analysis to be used in a meaningful way, the economic data must accurately reflect the range of monetary transactions that take place within the local economy. The previous chapter discussed briefly data collection in the context of market research. The same principles apply. The first stage is to identify what local economic data already exists and in what form.

Table 25:

The Tourism Multiplier in Action

	Action	Expenditure	Income
1.	*A family spends in a hotel*	£500	
2.	*The hotel in turn spends this money on:*		
	Purchases of goods and services	255	
	VAT	75	
	Taxes	45	
	Rates	10	
	Wages and profit locally	**115**	*Direct Income*
3.	*The suppliers spend their income on:*	65	
	Goods for resale, and	30	
	Other services	15	
	Taxes	5	
	Rates	5	
	Wages and profit locally	**10**	*Generated Spending*
4.	*Direct and Generated Income*	**125**	
	of this £105 is re-spent	**105**	
5.	*Additional Income*	**20**	*Additional Income*
	TOTAL INCOME =	**145**	
	For every £500 spent by a visitor, £145 is generated as additional income so in this case the multiplier would be 0.29.	145	
		500	

Any new data should provide information that will clearly show the impact of tourism spending within the local economy. Such surveys must cover a representative sample of the visitor and local business population and be undertaken over a sufficiently long time-scale to reflect any seasonal or cyclical elements in spending patterns.

Because of the need for highly accurate data at a disaggregated level, such studies using multiplier analysis are usually confined to a local or sub-regional level. They involve time-consuming interviews and visitor surveys and would be expensive to replicate on a larger scale. For this reason, studies of the economic impact of tourism at a national or supra-national level have used different measures.

2. Tourism Impacts on National or Supra-national Economies

Tourism as an economic activity at national level is generally measured using three criteria:
— its contribution to overall economic activity;
— its contribution to overall employment;
— its contribution to the Balance of Payments.

(a) Contribution to Overall Economic Activity

The two most useful measures are the ratio of tourist receipts (income) with Gross Domestic Product and tourist expenditures with Private Final Consumption. The tourist receipts of a country generate economic activity and are therefore a measure of economic production of that country. Tourist expenditures (i.e. consumption) are part of the overall consumption (Private Final Consumption). Not all countries or tourist regions possess economic data that accurately measure these components, but the annual reports of the OECD on *Tourism Policy and International Tourism* contain a wide range of economic data for the member countries, that can be used to calculate the proportion of tourist income and expenditure compared with total income and expenditure.

Between 1975 and 1985 the proportion of international tourist receipts in the GDP of the OECD member countries has increased steadily, particularly in the United States, Germany and Spain. Within the Common Market countries total tourist receipts were of most importance in France (over 5% of GDP), Greece (over 4%) and West Germany (over 4%).

International tourist expenditures as a component of Private Final Consumption was most important in Germany (over 4%), Denmark (4%), Ireland (4%) and the Netherlands (over 4%) and least important in Greece (1.1%), (OECD 1985). However, the income and expenditure from international tourism is only part of total tourist activity. In order to calculate the total contribution to overall economic activity it is necessary to collect data on.

— international tourist income and expenditure;
— intra and extra-regional tourist income and expenditure;
— domestic tourist income and expenditure.

Moreover, estimates based on direct contributions of tourist spending do not provide a complete picture. Tourist spending makes an indirect contribution to economic activity as the initial incomes are re-spent within the national economy.

(b) Contribution to Employment

It is difficult to measure the total number of jobs dependent on or generated by the tourist industry, as the effects of spending by tourists are seen across a wide range of occupations and are felt directly and indirectly. There are three particular problems when relating tourism to employment:

(i)   The tourist product is very diversified and covers a wide range of economic activities, many of which provide services used by the local population. Thus censuses of employment usually include hotels with restaurants and other catering and do not distinguish between those firms mainly servicing the tourist and those who do not. Transport is often put as a single category without the tourism element being identified.

(ii) Employment statistics tend to cover employees only and often fail to register employers or self-employed. Many tourism businesses are small businesses run by families or owner-managers and they make up a major proportion of total employment in the industry.

(iii) Tourism is a seasonal activity and its importance as an employer will fluctuate with the seasonal changes in visitor numbers.

Most studies linking tourism to employment are based on expenditure data for three sectors of the economy:

— direct employment in businesses that sell goods and services directly to the tourist;

— indirect employment in manufacturing and wholesale distribution firms that supply goods and services to tourism businesses;

— employment in construction industries (investment-related employment). (A. Smaoui).

In the United Kingdom the earnings from tourism have increased steadily since the mid-1970s, and studies of direct and indirect tourist spending suggest that jobs in the main tourism sectors have grown by 22% between 1975 and 1985 to just over 1.25 million. (Action for Jobs in Tourism 1986). Over the same period employment in manufacturing fell by 26% and jobs in the service sector generally grew by 9%. During a period of limited economic growth, tourism has performed very favourably in creating jobs compared with other sectors of the economy.

(c) Contribution to the Balance of Payments

A country such as Britain receives a significant income from spending by overseas tourists. For example, in 1985 14.5 million overseas visitors spent £5.5 billion. This is known as an 'invisible export', as it contributes to the national economy. However in the same year around 6.5 million Britons took holidays abroad spending money on tourist goods and services in other countries and they were therefore 'importing' these services. The contribution of tourism to the overall balance of payments of a country is the *difference* between the amount which overseas visitors spend in the country and the amount that the country's residents spend overseas, and shows the net surplus or deficit on the tourism account. Figure 27 on page 136 shows the contribution of tourism to the balance of payments between 1975 and 1987.

In developing countries with limited potential for exporting manufactured goods and reliant on low cost primary products, and imported high-cost products, the development of tourist facilities can greatly improve their balance of payments position by bringing a considerable inflow of spending into the local economy. In this context tourism can have a stabilising effect by decreasing a deficit on their overall balance of payments.

Most Communist bloc countries have tried to encourage the inflow of Western tourists whilst placing restrictions on the foreign travel of their own nationals, with the aims of improving their balance of payments and 'importing' much needed hard currency.

As well as influencing the creation of jobs and general trade balance at national level, tourism can make an important economic impact at regional level. 'Region' in this context can mean part of a country, or an individual country that is part of an economic trading bloc. In regions with scarce national resources and limited

135

Figure 28 : Balance of expenditure between Overseas Visitors to the United Kingdom(+) and UK Visitors Overseas (−) at constant (1980) prices

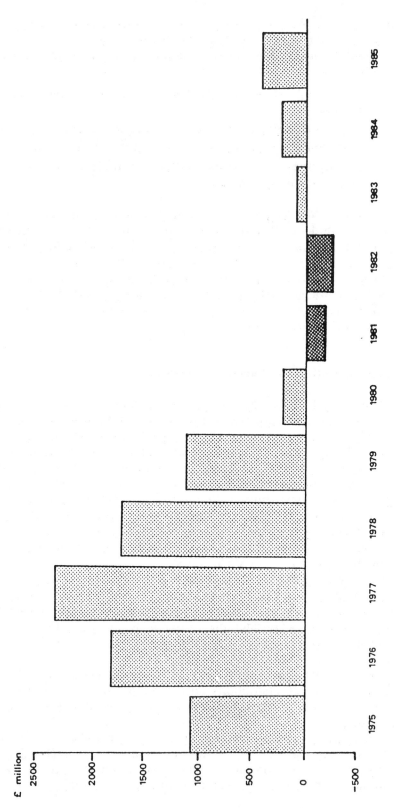

SOURCE: International Passenger Survey

manufacturing potential and where agriculture may be marginal, tourism is often seen as a major catalyst in the development process.

The example of Languedoc-Roussillon in Chapter 9 is a good example of the way in which tourism development can transform a hitherto under-developed region. The economy of the region was mainly agricultural, largely low quality wine production, and rural depopulation was occurring at a rapid rate. Over £600 million was invested in a tourism development programme during the 1970s and 1980s. 30,000 year round and 20,000 seasonal jobs were created in providing direct tourist services, ancilliary services, and construction/public works. Over 8 million visitors a year spend over £66 million in the region.

ASSIGNMENTS

1. Using sets of data from a recent OECD annual report on tourism policy and international tourism:
   (a) Assess the impact of tourism on the economies of 4 contrasting member states.
   (b) Plot the balance of payments 1975—1985 for two member states.

2. Using the further reading referred to in the text, critically review the application of multiplier analysis to the study of at least *one* local economy.

Chapter 12
Tourism Impact Studies
2: The Impact of Tourism on the Environment

Learning Objectives. After reading this chapter and the references contained within it you should have a clear understanding of:

— the types of impact that can occur;
— the methods of measuring the impacts of tourism development upon the environment;
— policy measures that have been developed to conserve the environment;
— methods of planning and managing tourism to reconcile conservation and development.

Introduction

There has been a growing awareness of the socio-cultural and environmental impacts of tourism on a region, and that disbenefits can occur through developments, which are often overlooked in the search for economic benefits of tourism. The large-scale seasonal influx of visitors can mean that by sheer pressure of numbers, the visitors to fragile environments risk destroying the very attractions that they come to see. In coastal regions the rapid growth of a tourist infrastructure in the form of hotels, condiminiums, shopping malls and roads, can transform a landscape in a short space of time. Because any discussion on the environmental impacts of tourism can risk being influenced by value-judgements, it is necessary to adopt an objective approach when measuring impacts. This chapter therefore seeks to describe and explain the types of impact that can occur, the methods of measuring these impacts, the public policy response (in the form of planning and control measures) that has evolved to conserve the environment, and management approaches designed to reconcile the inherent conflict between conservation and development.

Types of Environmental Impact

Tourism impacts on the environment in a number of ways. There is the visual intrusion of large numbers of parked and moving vehicles; the presence of large numbers of people on beaches or footpaths or lakesides. There is noise, pollution and overcrowding. There is destruction of vegetation, visual intrusion of new buildings; developments out of scale with existing buildings. There is the impact on the vegetation and the wildlife; and the impact on the ecological system as a whole. Overall there is a very real risk that if unchecked, tourism development will lead to conflicts over the use of land.

For example in the coastal dune areas of North West England, and on the coasts of Holland and Denmark, trampling has caused the loss of stabilising vegetation leading to sand blows inland, the collapse of a fragile ecosystem and the inundation of farmland. In the Dutch dune system, because of its importance as a sea defence, no public access is allowed to beaches except on a few board walks. In Norway and Sweden the increasing spread of second homes in the mountain areas which lack sewage systems has led to pollution of local rivers and streams, (Council of Europe 1971).

The nature of the tourism impacts is associated with the nature of the tourist resources. With natural resources i.e. beaches, national parks, lakesides or forests, it is the ability of the resource to absorb the tourist that is the first measure of impact. This has been measured in relation to the *capacity* of the resource. There are three different kinds of capacity: physical, environmental and ecological.

Physical Capacity is the easiest concept to grasp because many tourist facilities/resources will have absolute limits on the number of tourists they can accommodate. Usually other constraints will intervene before this is reached. For example the approach roads will become congested or car parks full before the beach reaches its maximum capacity.

Environmental Capacity. This is the maximum level of tourist use that an area can accommodate before visitors perceive a decline in their attraction to that place and move on elsewhere. This is the most abstract and least tangible measure of capacity, but is an important influence on visitor behaviour. This level of capacity is very personal and varies with the season, prevailing weather, and type of tourist activity — so a wide range of capacity levels exist using this as a measure. Burton (1974) in her work on Cannock Chase established that 10 to 50 cars in sight represented a critical level of use at which people first perceived the environment was crowded.

This concept has been studied in different tourist environments to produce national standards of capacity. Dower and McCarthy (1967) in their study of Donegal identified a range of resources critical to the development of tourism and estimated the capacity of each to take people at any one time. Using studies by Furmidge (1969) Houghton-Evans and Miles (1970) it is possible to produce a range of estimates of environmental capacity, see Table 26 below:

Table 26:
Suggested Space Standards for Environmental Capacity

Type of recreation area	National environmental capacity
Major scenic route	20 persons per mile
Minor scenic route	4 persons per mile
Major scenic feature	20 persons per mile
Major historic site	30 persons per mile
Woodland area	100 persons per square mile
Picnic area	60 persons
Enclosed land	50 persons per square mile
Rough or hill land	5 persons per square mile
Coast or lake shore (basic level)	50 persons per mile
Attractive and accessible coast/beach	400 persons per mile

Ecological Capacity is the maximum level of tourist use that an area can accommodate before ecological damage or decline occurs. It is affected by geology, soils, vegetation cover and terrain of an area and the seasonal intensity of tourist use. A person on horseback has more effect than one on foot. When people come in vehicles, especially the 4-wheel drive variety which gives them much greater accessibility to fragile landscapes, the wheels of these vehicles can destroy the vegetation cover and expose heath and stone. This has happened in parts of the New Forest where damage to the vegetation and to trees has occurred, and access to water and food for wild animals has been restricted.

In her work *The Recreational Carrying Capacity of the Countryside* (Burton 1974) Rosemary Burton points out that because the concept of carrying capacity is little understood and because it has not been translated into a set of practical planning guidelines, attempts to manage environmentally sensitive areas are often frustrated. Although this work was undertaken over 15 years ago, the findings are just as relevant today because of the continuing need to understand and plan for the impacts of tourism on the environment.

Case Studies of Environmental Impact

1. Spain

In the 1950s and 1960s, Spain was developed as a major destination for mass market package tours. By the late 1970s, the growth of domestic and international tourism produced a seasonal influx of over 56 million tourists, concentrated parts of its Mediterranean coast.

The Spanish authorities, when faced with this huge inflow of seasonal visitors, took two policy decisions. First, they sought to maximise the income from tourism. Secondly, they wished to minimise the damage to the environment. In order to assess the nature, scale, and distribution of tourism impact, several studies were carried out during the 1970s to measure:

— the capacity of the tourist regions;
— the existing levels of tourist use of these regions (i.e. their market share).

The aim was to identify those tourist regions with the greatest pressures of visitor use.

The tourist capacity of the leading holiday regions was calculated using the following formula:

$$\text{Tourist Capacity} = \frac{\text{No. of Beds} + \text{No. of Restaurants} + \text{No. of Commercial Licences}}{\text{Normal Population ('000's)} \times \text{Land area (Km}^2)} \times 100$$

This index produced the following table of leading tourist regions:

Region	Tourist Capacity	Rank
Costa Brava	27.7	1
Majorca	13.6	2
Costa del Sol	10.5	3
Grand Canary Island	8.0	4
Barcelona	6.7	5
Madrid	4.5	6
Murica-Alicante	3.6	7
Tenerife	2.3	8
San Sebastian	2.0	9
Santander	1.0	10

This can then be related to the market share of the various regions as a proportion of total tourists to Spain.

Region	Market Share (%)	Rank
Majorca	35.2	1
Murica-Alicante	7.4	2
Madrid	7.5	3
Barcelona	6.8	4
Costa del Sol	6.4	5
Costa Brava	5.5	6
Tenerife	5.1	7
Great Canary Islands	4.7	8
Santander	0.8	9
San Sebastian	0.7	10

It can be seen from this limited example that some regions with a more limited tourist capacity (such as Murica-Alicante) had a greater market share than other regions such as Grand Canary which posessed greater capacity. Certain localities such as Murica-Alicante or the Costa del Sol were faced with a substantial influx of tourists over a limited period in the year and this led to a range of problems including acute congestion specially on the coastal strip, inadequate infrastructure, environmental damage and overloading of local services. Recent publicity has highlighted the response of the Spanish authorities to the spread of development especially on the coastal strip of the Costa del Sol, where now new development is to be allowed within 100 metres of the shoreline and buildings erected without planning permission may be demolished.

2. Languedoc-Roussillon

The development of this stretch of the South of France was described in detail in Chapter 9. Over a period of 20 years a 180 kilometre stretch of the French Mediterranean coast was transformed from a remote rural region of lakes, salt marshes and uninterrupted beaches into the second most important tourist region in France. There were few roads and the local infrastructure was limited. Six new resorts were built, with a total capacity of 2 million visitors and moorings for over 20,000 boats. A network of major roads and water supply installations were developed. Between the six resorts the natural vegetation and original landscape was to be preserved and protected so that the local flora and fauna would remain.

However, tourism development on this scale will have a considerable impact on the environment. How do we measure this impact? Is it a beneficial impact or a detrimental one? Was the original environment worth preserving? How can we best plan for tourism development so as to minimise its impact on the environment? How can the remnants be best conserved? In any assessment of the impact of tourism on the environment these are some of the questions that must be answered.

Methods of Measuring Environmental Impact

The original work on environmental impact studies was developed in the United States, the stimulus being the *National Environmental Policy Act (1972)* which required Federal Authorities to identify and measure the environmental impacts of proposals and to disclose the results of State and local bodies and the public. Several methods of environmental impact analysis have been developed, and three of those most adaptable to measuring tourism impacts are outlined below.

(i) Overlays

This is the most simple method of EIA and consists of a series of map transparencies overlaid to show the geographic extent and intensity of impact of proposed developments. An area can be divided into grid squares and within each square information can be displayed showing the potential impact of development proposals on environmental factors. This can bring out significant conflicts between development and the environment. At a manual level there is a practical limit to the number of overlays that can be effectively superimposed upon one another. However, the use of computer graphics could overcome this problem and a wide range of overlays could be interrelated to identify interactions.

(ii) Matrices

A matrix can be constructed to show the impacts of the proposed developments (on the horizontal axis) on the individual characteristics of the existing tourist region (on the vertical axis). Within each cell of the matrix it is possible to assess the level of the individual impacts (Fig 28 on page 144) with a score ranging from 1 to 10 representing the increasing size or magnitude of the impact. For example a proposed hotel complex or condominium development might lower the existing water table by several inches, or introduce the risk of pollution within the network of local rivers and lakes. This would produce a high score as a measure of the environmental impact. One criticism of this method is that it only takes account of the *immediate* impacts and is not sufficiently sophisticated to account for secondary and successive levels of impact.

An impact matrix should take account of both the development and the operational phase of a tourism project and the scale of individual impacts may vary between these two phases. If at all possible impacts should be measured objectively using quantitative analysis so that the end product of an impact matrix would be a summary indicating that a proposed tourism development will produce:

— gains or losses;
— short term or long term effects;
— reversible or irreversible effects;
— local or regional impacts.

Models

The view that matrices are cumbersome to construct and only measure first order impacts led to the construction of dynmamic simulation models. The environment is seen as an open or closed *system* and models are constructed which predict the

Figure 29
Environmental Impact Analysis Matrix

OPERATIONAL PHASE

CHARACTERISTICS OF EXISTING SITUATION	Land Needs	Population Changes	Noise from plant	Traffic Noise	Transport of material	Pollution	Increased Traffic	Water Discharge	Transport of Employees	Labour Needs	Site use
SCENERY											
LAND USE											
RESIDENT POPULATION											
TOURIST POPULATION											
TRAFFIC MOVEMENT PATTERNS											
NOISE AND DISTURBANCE											
ECOLOGICAL CHARACTERISTICS											
ARCHAEOLOGICAL CHARACTERISTICS											
POLLUTION											
POWER SUPPLY											
SERVICES											
SEWERAGE											
EXISTING SETTLEMENT											

CONSTRUCTION PHASE

CHARACTERISTICS OF EXISTING SITUATION	Land Needs	Population Changes	Noise from plant	Traffic Noise	Transport of material	Pollution	Increased Traffic	Water Discharge	Transport of Employees	Labour Needs	Site use
SCENERY											
LAND USE											
RESIDENT POPULATION											
TOURIST POPULATION											
TRAFFIC MOVEMENT PATTERNS											
NOISE AND DISTURBANCE											
ECOLOGICAL CHARACTERISTICS											
ARCHAEOLOGICAL CHARACTERISTICS											
POLLUTION											
POWER SUPPLY											
SERVICES											
SEWERAGE											
EXISTING SETTLEMENT											

144

effects of changes brought about by tourism developments on this environment. The system can be seen at successive intervals of time as a series of calculations are carried out to predict successive impacts on the environment. The construction of such models generally requires considerable data about the environment and the proposed development, and this may require time and technical expertise that is not available. Provided such data is available it is possible to construct complex mathematical models to deal with large complex development proposals.

Policy Responses to Environmental Impact

With the growth in tourism on a world scale not only are more people using the coastal and inland regions for tourism, they are travelling greater distances, impacting on a greater area and spending more time there. Over the past 40 years there has been a increasing concern for the quality of this environment and the need to conserve scenery and wildlife in areas of great natural beauty. At the same time there have been growing demands for more land for urban development, for roads and factories, for water supply, mineral extraction and many other land uses. The remaining land must also be used for farming forestry and many other needs.

In order to meet these conflicting demands on the use of land and to conserve areas with fragile ecosystems or of great scenic value, most countries have developed a hierarchy of planning controls. The major landscape resources are conserved in *National Parks,* with the Yellowstone National Park in the USA the first to be established in 1872. The US *National Park Service Act* of 1916 sums up the role of National Parks

> *'to conserve the scenery and natural objects and wildlife therein, to provide for the enjoyment of the same, in such a manner and by such means as will leave them unimpaired for the enjoyment of future generations'.*

The Netherlands has three National Parks similar in concept to those of the United States. In Britain and West Germany by way of contrast most of the land in the National Parks is in private ownership and they have the normal land uses of farming, forestry and mineral extraction. In England and Wales the designation of an area as a National Park enables special planning legislation to be used to control use and development of this land. The National Park authorities have powers to plant trees, clear eyesores and provide facilities for tourists such as car parks, camp sites and information centres. Following the *National Parks and Access to the Countryside Act* of 1949, 10 National Parks were established in England and Wales. The 1949 Act also provided for the designation of Areas of Outstanding Natural Beauty (AONB's) of which 33 have now been recognised (Fig 29 on page 146). Following the 1968 *Countryside Act* local authorities in England and Wales have the powers to establish country parks and picnic sites. These are much smaller but nevertheless attractive recreational facilities and are sited in pleasant countryside within easy access of the major conurbations. One underlying reason for their establishment was a belief that they would help to relieve pressure from the National Parks which were faced with a growing influx

Figure 30 : **National Parks, AONB's and Stretches of Heritage Coast in England & Wales**

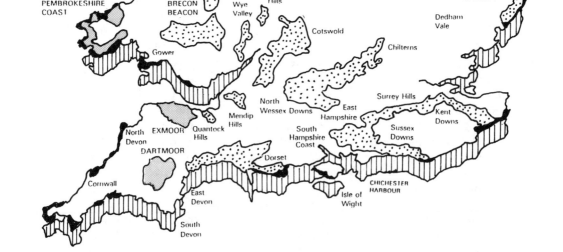

Legend:
- National Parks
- Areas of Outstanding Natural Beauty
- Heritage Coasts

Northumberland coast
Solway Coast
NORTHUMBERLAND
Lake District
Arnside & Silverdale
NORTH YORK MOORS
Forest of Bowland
YORKSHIRE DALES
Anglesey
PEAK DISTRICT
Lincolnshire Wolds
Lleyn
SNOWDONIA
Cannock Chase
Norfolk Coast
Shropshire Hills
Malvern Hills
Suffolk Coast & Heaths
PEMBROKESHIRE COAST
BRECON BEACON
Wye Valley
Cotswold
Dedham Vale
Gower
Chilterns
North Wessex Downs
Surrey Hills
Kent Downs
Mendip Hills
East Hampshire
North Devon
EXMOOR
Quantock Hills
South Hampshire Coast
Sussex Downs
DARTMOOR
Dorset
CHICHESTER HARBOUR
Cornwall
East Devon
Isle of Wight
South Devon

of car owning visitors who could reach with ease the remoter more fragile landscape areas.

The most successful examples of conservation are in the United States and Holland where land ownership and management are in the hands of one Authority. In Britain, a quasi-public body the National Trust has acquired many thousands of acres of countryside and coast and protects them in the face of development pressures. Otherwise in Britain the National Parks have a chequered history as a means of controlling land use, especially mineral extraction.

The most successful measures to reconcile tourism development with environmental conservation have come about through the development of management plans for tourist regions. Conservation is the sensible use of resources and is concerned with the quality and the quantity of many resources. Underlying this is a general view that if the natural resources are not conserved, they will deteriorate or be destroyed and then the tourists will leave perhaps never to return. This could have disastrous effects on a local, regional, or national economy.

Planning for Tourist Environments

The ecological, scenic and social impacts of tourism can be both positive and negative. The key to successful integration of tourism in the environment lies in planning and management of any proposed development. The aim must be to use rural and coastal resources so that as many demands as possible can be provided for. A number of management techniques must be used to minimise existing conflicts and to conserve the environment for future generations to use and enjoy.

In order to protect those regions with scarce or fragile environments a threefold planning programme needs to be agreed. This consists of:

(i)   increasing the capacity of regions/resources already committed to tourist use;

(ii) creating new resources for tourism using reclaimed or undeveloped and disused land around our cities;

(iii) developing multiple use of the same resource.

(i)   Increasing the Capacity of Existing Sites/Regions

Wherever possible the aim should be to improve the capacity of existing resorts and holiday areas to accommodate more tourism. This will involve a reappraisal of the use and effectiveness of existing resources and the development of management measures outlined later in this chapter. The advantage with this approach is that these destinations are already well known to the public and are likely to receive the first impact of any increase in demand for tourism. As demand and therefore use is often seasonal, measures to extend the season can also help to minimise peak season congestion.

(ii) Creation of New Tourist Resources

This can take 2 forms:

(a)   the reclamation of land from the sea by means of polder or barrage schemes;

(b)   the development of derelict or under-used land around our major towns and cities, especially in or adjacent to the main tourist destinations.

The reclamation of the Ijsselmeer and the Delta scheme in Holland have created a great number of new tourist opportunities for camping, water sports and natural history. The proposed barrage schemes for Morecambe Bay and the Wash in England and in Southern France would also provide new resources for water-based tourism activities.

Throughout Europe there are many thousands of hectares of disused mineral workings, former railways, derelict canals and disused airfields that can be reclaimed/redeveloped for tourism uses. Sand and gravel workings can be reclaimed for water-based tourism. Many of the country parks in Britain and the regional parks in France include derelict mineral workings or industrial land that has been reclaimed. In Britain disused railways have been converted into long distance footpaths and bridleways and disused canals have been restored and now provide facilities for cruising, walking and other activities. Much of the derelict industrial land and mineral workings is within easy access of major towns and cities, and if it can be reclaimed and put to tourist uses, this will help to relieve the pressures on the more distant, perhaps more fragile, environments. The recent developments in some of Britain's inner city areas are a case in point. In London the 9-mile stretch of former docklands is being transformed as part of a major development project to provide a wealth of man-made and water-based tourist at-tractions. Similar, but smaller scale schemes are under way in the dockland areas of Bristol, Liverpool, Swansea, Hull and Newcastle.

However, reclamation of underused land or restoration of derelict land is not the only answer, and may not be possible in every case. In order to protect and conserve the environment it is also necessary to integrate tourism with other land uses especially water supply, afforestation and nature conservation.

(iii)   Multiple Use

The reservoirs and their catchments in upland Britain can serve as visitor attrac-tions and provide opportunities for walking, sailing, camping and fishing. The Kielder scheme is a good example, where a major new tourism development scheme is under way. 8 projects are planned in a 2-year programme centred on Kielder water and the surrounding forest area. Additional sports facilities, provi-sion of more accommodation, improving existing facilities are part of an am-bitious development plan jointly sponsored by the Forestry Commission, the Sports Council, the Water Authority and the local authorities.

In Britain, the Forestry Commission has successfully integrated tourism with forestry and now provides opportunities for many activities including scenic drives, picnic sites, camping and fishing. Britain now has seven Forest Parks where these activities are encouraged, and in parts of upland Britain the Forestry Commission has developed and built holiday villages. In the Netherlands over 10% of the holdings of the state forest service are managed for tourism and the service has built roads, camp-sites, viewpoints and picnic areas. In the United States many of the forest areas in the National Parks play a similar role and see no conflict between the need for timber supply and the provision of amenities for tourists.

148

Managing Tourist Environments

The most effective means of resolving potential conflicts between tourism and the environment is by applying good management practice. In this context three aspects of management are involved:

    (i)   traffic management;

    (ii)   land management;

    (iii)   visitor management.

(i)   Traffic Management

Tourists often travel by car to or within their holiday destination, and the large numbers of moving and parked cars are one of the most immediate impacts of tourism on the environment. For many years traffic management has been recognised as a necessary means of controlling the movement and access of vehicles in major towns and cities. In tourist regions the same principles will need to be applied if the impact of traffic is to be minimised. This should take the form of traffic design and highway engineering. Traffic design includes the provision of one-way systems, speed limits, limits to access to the remoter areas. In some areas cars may be banned altogether. In the Peak District National Park an experiment was carried out in the Goyt Valley where rural roads were closed at weekends to all vehicles except minibuses carrying visitors into the valley from car parks located around its perimeter (Miles 1972). This scheme was possible because the valley had limited access by road and had no resident population.

To compensate for restrictions on motor vehicles the planning authorities should provide scenic drives, picnic areas and viewpoints at other locations. In some cases new roads may need to be build by-passing environmentally sensitive areas. The Susten Pass in Switzerland between Innertkirchan and Wassen and the Deutsch Weinstrasse from the French border to Mainz are good examples of such purpose-built routes.

(ii)   Land Management

This concerns aspects of design and maintenance, and by a mix of persuasion and financial incentives encouraging private bodies to provide amenities for tourists on their land. A circulation pattern may be necessary to direct and control the flow of visitors through a site and this may involve the erection of signs, fences and barriers, additional landscaping and planting schemes. It may be necessary to change the visitor access points and circulation routes on an annual basis to minimise the effects of trampling on the vegetation and to introduce a programme of planned maintenance of the site. It is important to know the number of visitors the site can support before the services in the form of car parking, access, water and sewage disposal risk becoming overloaded. There is a need, therefore, to monitor visitor numbers so that controls can be introduced if overcrowding or congestion can be prevented. Good visitor management techniques are essential in order to control the impact of tourism on the environment.

(iii)   Visitor Management

The most effective techniques of visitor management are usually unobtrusive but persuasive. Visitor management involves two actions — preventing or restricting access to environmentally fragile areas and directing visitors to those areas that can accommodate them. The most immediate control on site usage can be by limiting car parking provision, since in Europe and the USA most tourists will use their car to visit the coast or countryside and most stay close to their car when they arrive there. In the Huron-Clinton system of regional parks around Detroit there is a system of notifying potential visitors that a park is 'full' and most Americans appear to be prepared to move on when they know a park is full.

Management by price is another control mechanism particularly for the private sector. A variation of this approach is to have a variable system of pricing related to the seasons, and prevailing visitor numbers.

The use of barriers such as ditches or screens of trees or mounds can deter people and when combined with direction signs to the visitor attractions control the spread of visitors in a recreational area. A scheme for the interpretation of the site is an essential element in the approach to visitor management. Guided tours or walks, exhibitions, self-guided trails or guide leaflets can all be used to guide visitors to those parts of the site that can accommodate them. If the tourist resource is sufficiently large it may be possible to zone different localities for a range of uses — from the intensive gregarious activities around the main beach/lakeside area — to the less gregarious scenic drives or small picnic areas and the remoter parts accessible on foot and some distance from the main visitor facilities.

In order for these planning and management measures to succeed, there is a need for continued coordination of efforts between central and local government and between the public and private sector. In many cases, the works needed to conserve the natural environment and to manage it effectively require capital investment from central government if they are to succeed. This raises issues related to the capital cost of financing of tourist developments, especially in National Parks and scenically important countryside and coastal areas, and the revenue costs of managing them. Should the tourist generating areas (i.e. the major towns and cities) pay for the upkeep of the rural recreation areas that they use and rely on? In the public sector should site management costs be financed by admission charges so that the burden of maintaining and conserving sites rests on those who use them? In the not too distant future we may have to find the answers to these and other difficult questions if our environment is to be preserved for future generations. The popularity and success of many private sector visitor attractions does indicate the ability and willingness of people to pay. These are complex issues and no clear cut solution has as yet emerged.

ASSIGNMENTS

1. Using a country park, stretch of coastline or beauty spot in your locality attempt to measure the following:

    (i)   the impact of visitors on the area;
    (ii)   the types of visitor amenities/facilities provided and their location;
    (iii)   the local policies for visitor management.

2. Using the reports of the National Park planning authorities in Britain, compare the approach to the *planning* and *management* in any 2 National Parks in Britain.

Chapter 13

New Developments in Tourism

Learning Objectives: After reading this chapter and the additional references you should have an understanding of:

— innovations in tourism development;
— the factors influencing the changing preferences of tourists;
— the tourist potential of our industrial heritage;
— new approaches to the tourist market.

Innovation is perhaps the one word that best describes the development of tourism in the 1980s and which separates this period from the main phases of expansion in the late 19th Century or the 1950s and 1960s. In North America and Europe the traditional tourist market is approaching saturation point and the major companies are competing for a market share of a relatively static market. In this kind of business environment it is the innovative entrepreneur, that can identify new resources and/or new preferences for tourists, who will become the market leader. This chapter attempts to identify new and emerging trends in tourism and discusses the lessons to be learned from them.

Innovations in Tourism Development

The traditional image of a tourist destination is a resort town set amidst attractive scenery with a variety of day-trip opportunities within easy access. The resort has been usually on the coast and has relied on sun, sea and sand to attract its clientele. During the 1970s and 1980s new types of tourist destinations have emerged. These are based on several types of product and demonstrate new approaches to tourism marketing.

This chapter examines how new tourism products have been developed and their role in helping to promote new tourist destinations, particularly areas not traditionally associated with tourism. In particular we examine:-

(i)   Open Air Museums/Industrial Heritage Areas;
(ii)   Inner city redevelopment, especially dockland projects;
(iii) The Garden Festival Concept;
(iv)   Theme Parks;
(v)   Time-Share;
(vi)   Leisure and speciality shopping in indoor resort complexes;
(vii) The High-Tech revolution that is affecting the industry.

(i)   Open Air Museums/Industrial Heritage Areas

The long-term decline in manufacturing in Europe and North America since the early 20th Century has left us with a rich heritage in industrial artefacts. Many of them are buildings and structures that are worthy of preservation in their own right. Some, because of their historic associations or their setting are worthy of preservation and interpretation for the benefit of future generations. Many local authorities have come to recognise the tourist potential of their industrial heritage provided the product is developed to a level where it would benefit from major promotion.

The North of England Open Air Museum at Beamish in County Durham is a case in point. This was one of the forerunners of a new museums movement designed to be a living museum recreating an industrial and social environment present in the region between 50 and 100 years ago. The museum occupies 300 acres and has a farm with live exhibits, an adit mine, a working tramway, steam railway and a village made up of buildings rescued from demolition from various sites in North East England. In a row of miners cottages on the site there are reconstructions of interiors common 50 years ago. In the West Midlands in 1967 the Ironbridge Gorge Museum was set up to preserve the industrial artefacts of Coalbrookdale which was one of the leading centres of the early industrial revolution. Now the Ironbridge Museum has an extensive open air site at Blists Hill, together with exhibits on several other sites in the locality.

In West Gwent the decline of coal mining, for so long synonymous with South Wales, led to a diversification into other newer types of industry and the rapid disappearance of the traditional mining landscape. The development of the Big Pit Mining Museum at Blaenavon was the result of an ambitious £1¼ million development to focus on the region's industrial heritage as a means of attracting tourists to the area.

Although each of these innovations has produced a new major tourist attraction, on its own, it is not sufficient as a catalyst for tourist development. Recent trends in tourism have included more short-break holidays and second and third holidays and a growth in study, countryside and activity holidays. In order to attract this potential market the tourist authorities associated with industrial heritage projects need to develop the tourist product as a whole. Because they are not traditional tourist regions most of these areas lack a range of adequate accommodation and lack information centres to provide a network of information. This means investment in major hotel schemes, development advice schemes for small businesses and establishing a network of information centres. Given this degree of commitment from local planning authorities and regional trust boards, there is a growing realisation of the potential of the industrial heritage for short-break and special interest holidays. In a rather unique way the Civil War battlefield sites in the United States and related locations such as Harpers Ferry VA, can be regarded as open air museums which attempt to faithfully replicate the major conflicts of the American Civil War. They are a major visitor attraction and now have visitor centres, battlefield drives and souvenir shops.

(ii) Inner City Tourism

(A) Waterfront Developments

The industrial heritage theme is also seen in the various dockland development projects under way in various parts of Britain. London, Bristol and Liverpool have extensive dockland areas full of empty industrial buildings and wasteland. In each case the public sector has played a key role in promoting private developments, and follows from the experience of similar projects in the United States. In 1977 the US Government passed the *Housing and Community Development* Act which was designed to assist severely distressed city communities containing pockets of poverty and facing economic deterioration. A programme of public and private investment was developed, and by 1982 over $2.2 billion of federal aid has been spent on the Urban Development Action Grants Programme. Perhaps the best known of the US projects was the revitalising of the inner Harbour area of Baltimore. The Harbour Place development has transferred a decaying derelict harbour area into a major tourist attraction, and a thriving commercial and conference location.

In London the regeneration of London Docklands involves an ambitious project covering over 9 miles of riverside land and four main sites — the Surrey Docks, Wapping, the Isle of Dogs and the Royal Docks. The government is spending over £446 million to provide a new infrastructure including a light railway, new roads, riverbus services and a short take off and landing (STOL) London City Airport. The private sector is expected to invest about £2.1 billion.

The existing waterscape of the docklands will be used as a backcloth for a mix of commercial, residential, retail and leisure development. New museums are planned for the area including a Victorian Life Museum and the Great Eastern Railway collection in the Royal Docks. There will also be a 25,000 seat Sports Stadium and education centre and a leisure complex. Marina developments will encourage sailing, windsurfing and waterskiing. The planting of thousands of trees, the development of riverside footpaths and new retail/leisure complexes will transform this part of London by the year 2,000.

On Merseyside the development of the region was initiated in the 1980s with the establishment of the Merseyside Development Corporation, the development of an Enterprise Zone and Freeport and Urban Development Grants. Within the Enterprise Zone (the Isle of Dogs in London's Dockland has a similar designation) there is up to 100% capital allowance against corporate taxes for capital expenditure on construction, exemption from local rates until 1992 and no planning permission required for developments which conform to the published scheme. Central government urban programme funds were used to attract private finance in joint ventures to develop Beatle City (£1 million) and the refurbishment of the Adelphi Hotel. The Merseyside Development Corporation has invested several million pounds in the South Docks providing an infrastructure that will in turn attract private investment. The Merseyside Maritime Museum alone received a third of the capital budget of the County Council 1984—5. A major proposal in the Albert Dock is for the Northern Tate Gallery. The Arrowcroft Group are investing substantial sums in the Albert Dock in mixed office and residential development. All of these proposals are designed to provide a new environment for tourism and the arts by investing in the rich industrial and maritime history of Merseyside.

The English Tourist Board recognised the potential of inner city waterfront sites and sought to act as a catalyst for change following the experience of North America in the 1960s and 1970s. There Baltimore's inner harbour, New York's South Street and Toronto's harbourfront have been transformed through mixed developments bringing in speciality shopping, entertainments, conference facilities and hotels. In Toronto 100 acres of disused derelict harbourfront have been converted into a new residential and marketplace area. In Australia in 1984 the New South Wales government announced the redevelopment of the Darling harbour area as part of a $2 billion (Australian) project. Based on the Baltimore model a festival marketplace has been built with a new exhibition centre, a maritime museum and a memorial link with downtown Sydney. The scheme has achieved in 5 years what it took Baltimore 12 to do. Already more than 2 million people have visited it and the scheme will employ 10,000.

In the U.K. there are currently about 30 waterfront projects under way. As well as London and Merseyside referred to earlier, Southampton has two major projects — a £200 million Ocean Village scheme and a £30 million Town Quay scheme. Ocean Village has already attracted over 1.75 million visitors and created 500 jobs. Portsmouth is developing its historic dockyard area as part of a Tourism Development Action Programme. This includes the historic naval dockyard, the Royal Navy Museum, HMS Victory, Warrior and the Mary Rose Museum.

Many other examples of waterfront schemes can be cited — such as Gloucester Docks where the National Waterways Museum and a £35 million speciality shopping and residential complex is due for completion in 1991. In Birmingham the Bridley Place waterfront development will include a convention centre, gardens, an hotel and festival marketplace. At Swansea and Hull ambitious marina and harbourfront residential developments/conversions are under way.

(B) Other Inner City Initiatives

In February 1989 the English Tourist Board announced a major programme to use tourism as a means of regenerating inner cities. This scheme had 3 main aims:

(i)   to create local partnerships dedicated to inner city redevelopment;

(ii)   to get key tourism development projects off the ground;

(iii) to give practical guidance on how a wide range of local interests can become involved in the tourism industry.

The English Tourist Board took the view that tourism in London and the south east was approaching saturation point and that the future of the industry relied on the expansion of tourism throughout the country. They felt that tourism needs to be seen as an important element in city plans so that inner cities are seen as places that people will visit for leisure and tourism, because their environments are pleasant to look at and they contain a wealth of tourist attractions. One such example is in the West Midlands where the Black Country Development Corporation, the Heart of England Tourist Board and the English Tourist Board have helped to raise the area's profile and attract investment. One of the joint venture projects under way is the Sandwell Mall on a former 125 acre steelworks site at Wednesbury where a £300 million retail and leisure complex is being built which will include hotels, department stores and a variety of leisure facilities employing up to 800 people.

(iii) The Garden Festival Concept

Garden Festivals began in Germany in the 1950s and have been held there regularly since then. In 1980 a festival was held in Montreal. These festivals take part in parks especially created for the occasion and which will remain afterwards as an area of enhanced landscape capable of attracting new investment. In Germany garden festivals (which last for six months) typically attract between 4 and 8 million visitors. In the 1983 Munich festival over 10 million visitors came to the festival.

In 1986 the National Garden Festival was held at Stoke-on-Trent based on the 164 acre site of a former steelworks closed in 1979. The site was within half a mile of the city centre and had direct access to the M6 motorway. A £9½ million reclamation scheme which involved extensive earthworks, landscaping and planting of over 180,000 trees and shrubs. A further £11 million was provided by the Department of the Environment and the City and County Councils to provide the structures, formal garden areas and exhibitions for the Garden Festival. Additional capital and revenue costs were to be met from sponsorship and gate receipts. The long-term aim was to provide an attractive infrastructure and landscape setting capable of attracting hotel, residential and major leisure development opportunities. The 1986 National Garden Festival acted as a catalyst for the long-term redevelopment of the site. Not only did it attract thousands of tourists into what may not be perceived as a tourist area, it also concentrated effort and resources, stimulated the local economy and is likely to bring long-term benefits to the area. Further garden festivals have been held in 1988 (Glasgow), and 1990 (Gateshead) and one is planned for 1992 (Wales). The lesson from the garden festivals to date is that they help focus the public attention on an unlikely tourist attraction which in itself is helping to transform and regenerate the local economy.

(iv) Theme Parks

These are perhaps epitomised by the Disneyland developments in California and more recently in Florida, where on several hundred acres of land a series of fantasy worlds has been created, together with rides and amusements and a wide range of fast food outlets capable of meeting the needs of tens of thousands of visitors in a single day. The development of a park on this scale is usually designed around a theme or themes. In Disneyland the themes are Adventureland, Main Street USA, New Orleans Square, Frontierland, Fantasyland and Tomorrowland, and the phenomenal success of this concept since its development in the late 1950s has spawned many imitations.

The forerunners of the theme parks in the USA were the seaside amusement parks such as Coney Island and Santa Cruz Beach boardwalk. In its first year of operation, in 1956, Disneyland attracted almost 4 million visitors and current visitor numbers are 12 million a year.

There are about 30 theme parks in the USA with a combined visitor level of 100 million per annum. The three Disney developments — Disneyland (California), Epcot Centre (Florida) and Walt Disney World (Orlando Florida) dominate the theme park market and between them account for over one-third of all visitors to USA theme parks. (See Figure 30).

Most USA theme parks were built in the period between 1950 and 1970 (Figure 31) with only two pre-dating this period of rapid growth. The situation has remained fairly static since the mid 1970s and visitor numbers have not grown

Figure 21

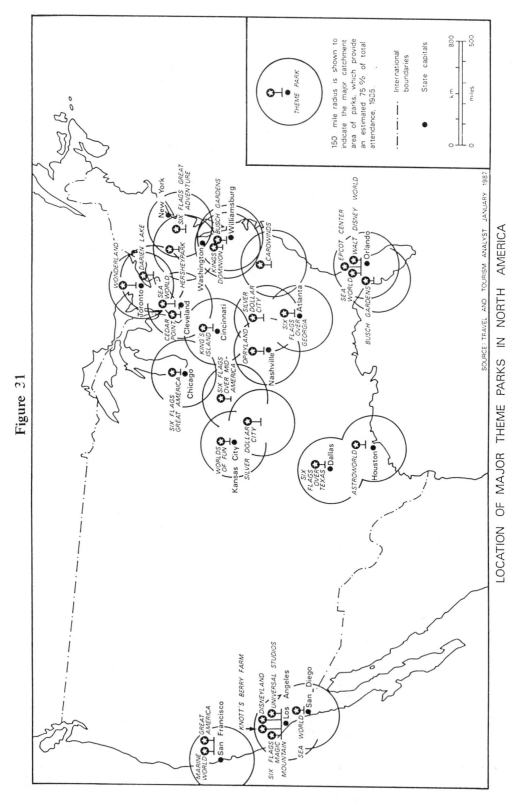

LOCATION OF MAJOR THEME PARKS IN NORTH AMERICA

substantially since then. The theme park market would appear to have reached saturation point, and many of the existing theme parks have concentrated on reinvestment, together with the development of indoor attractions.

USA theme park ownership is highly concentrated, with 21 of the 29 largest attractions owned by six companies. With corporate ownership they have been able to achieve levels of capital investment generally not available in Europe. Most US theme parks are visited by day trippers with most of their catchment coming from a 150 mile radius. In 1986 the US Travel Data Centre carried out a survey of 2,000 people regarding their frequency of visits to theme parks.

On the basis of this study, the International Association of Amusement Parks and Attractions estimated that 235 million visits would be made to major theme parks, smaller theme parks and amusement parks in 1986. This study also showed that visiting a theme park is an important element in holiday planning and two thirds of the sample said that such tourist attractions played a part in selecting a holiday destination.

Unlike the USA, in Europe theme parks have been going through a boom period in the 1980s. They are of much more recent origin, most having been created in the last 17 years. Most are concentrated in Northern Europe reflecting the concentration of populations and higher levels of car ownership and disposable income in countries such as Britain, Holland and West Germany.

The largest European theme park is De Efterling in the Netherlands which is a fantasy-based park with themes based on well-known fairy tales. In recent years several 'white knuckle' rides have been added. De Efterling attracts over 2 million visitors a year. The leading European theme park is Europa Park in West Germany between the Black Forest and Alsace. The park has a European theme with Italian and Dutch villages and French, German and Scandinavian themed areas. The 40 hectare site also has about 30 rides and facilities for entertainments in a 800 seat theatre.

The European theme parks, like their counterparts in the USA, predominantly attract day trippers. Between 70 and 95 per cent of all visitors to the main European theme parks are day visitors, and most have come from places within 2 hours journey time of the park.

Most of the new theme park developments are taking place in France, in part encouraged by Disney's announcement of plans to open a theme park near Paris in 1991. Two of the most recent developments: Mirapolis (opened in 1989 also north of Paris and costing £80 million) are seasonal operations. Only the Euro-Disney project will have a significant covered element to support year-round opening. The initial season for Mirapolis was disastrous and only a major reorganisation of its management and better budgeting and control have overcome a difficult start. (Leisure Management – January 1988). This experience does highlight the highly competitive nature of the theme park market and the need to exercise all round quality control and to ensure that the standards of the product, the landscaping and the rides are maintained as new theme parks come on to the market.

The first Disneyland in Europe is currently being developed at Marne la Vallee just 25 miles from Paris and the battle for the contract saw competing bids from Barcelona and Alicante in Spain. The reason for the fierce competition can be seen in the impact of a Disney theme park on the regional economy. The construction phase which will be from 1988 to the year 2000 will create 20,000 jobs and the running of the park another 30,000. 10 million visitors a year are expected, more than half of them Non-French (*The Times*). The new French Disneyland will have a French flavour alongside the planned Wild West and New Orleans Jazz areas.

The largest and best known theme park in Britain is Alton Towers in North Staffordshire which attracts over 1½ million visitors a year to the 700 acre site. There are over 200 acres of gardens and lakes, 300 acres of woodlands and a series of rides and attractions. Currently over £5 million is being invested in new rides for the 1987 season. The original house — Alton Towers is being restored and renovated and acts as a backcloth to the main fairground activities of the theme park. Alton Towers is located mid-way between the M6 and M1 motorways and has over 20 million people within 2 hours journey-time of the park.

These theme parks act as tourist 'honey pots' and by their sheer size and drawing power can attract visitors from a catchment up to a day's journey time. Often, as has happened in the United States, the presence of a major theme park will act as a spur to related tourist development particularly accommodation provision. The major drawback with Alton Towers as a tourist destination is the lack of adequate good quality accommodation in the immediate vicinity of the park.

By careful planning and design a large number of tourists can be managed and guided through the theme park in ways that were referred to in the previous chapter. The spread of rides and distribution of gift/craft shops, restaurants and fast food outlets can be built into the overall design of the theme park so that organised routes can be developed in an unobtrusive way.

The same company is now engaged in the transformation of the former Battersea Power Station into a massive leisure complex. This Grade II listed building, one of London's more unusual landmarks, is within easy access to central London which is already a major tourist destination.

(v)   Time Share

In the past the tradition has been for more prosperous individuals to buy or build second homes, and certain parts of France, Spain and Scandinavia became synonymous with widespread second home development. However, as these properties are often empty for part of the year they are costly to maintain and require payment of rates and taxes and risk being vandalised. As an alternative to this developers hit upon the concept of multi-ownership or time-sharing as a way of selling holiday apartments during the recession in the United States in the early 1970s. For a single capital outlay the buyer gets one or more weeks of fully furnished and equipped holiday accommodation for a given period of years. The cost of purchase varies with the holiday season, the most expensive weeks being at the optimum time of the season. There is also usually an annual maintenance charge.

Timeshare is one of the fastest growing sectors of the holiday market in the 1980s with much of the growth concentrated in the USA (850,000 timeshare owners) and Europe (32,000) especially in the UK, France, Italy and Switzerland. It represents a current investment of over £5 billion by 1.2 million owners worldwide *(Travel and Tourism Analyst)*.

Table 27 shows the growth of timeshare ownership over the period 1975 to 1985. In Asia it is almost entirely concentrated in Japan.

Table 27:
Growth of Timeshare Ownership 1975—1985

Nationality of Owner	1975	1980	1985
USA/Canada	5,000	260,000	650,000
Europe	15,000	70,000	220,000
Asia	35,000	50,000	160,000
Mexico	1,000	20,000	75,000
Africa	2,000	4,000	30,000
Caribbean	2,000	10,000	25,000
Central/South America	—	10,000	20,000
Australasia	—	5,000	20,000

Source: UK Tourism Advisory Group

The concept was further refined in the mid-1970s when salesmen found that while potential clients were attracted to particular timeshare accommodation, they did not wish to be tied to holidays in the same location year after year.

This led to the introduction of timeshare exchanges between different individuals in different resorts. There are now two main international timeshare exchange companies, Interval International and Resort Condominiums International which is by far the largest with 560,000 members in 1200 resorts in 70 countries. It was the emergence of these two companies which encouraged the rapid growth of timeshare developments from the mid-1970s onwards. The most recent development has been that of entire timeshare resorts. The Marriott Corporation have five timeshare resorts and is planning more. Club Hotel (a subsidiary of Club Mediterannee) in France with over 40 resorts is the market leader in Europe. Most of the timeshare properties in Europe are located around the shores of the Mediterranean, and in France and Italy most of the timeshare owners are nationals from within the domestic market. In Italy there are about 40,000 owners in 45 resorts — either in the ski-ing regions of the Alps or along the beaches of southern Italy. In the UK about 40,000 of the total 60,000 timeshare owners have bought weeks outside the UK, mainly in Spain and the Canaries. Table 28 outlines the major European timeshare companies.

Table 28:
Major Companies Developing Timeshare in Europe

Club Hotel (Club Mediterannee)	French	40,000 owners	40 resorts
Hapimag	Swiss	30,000 owners	48 resorts
Barratt	UK	10,000 owners	7 resorts
Incorporated Investments	UK	10,000 owners	2 resorts
Wimpey	UK	3,500 owners	5 resorts
Kenning Atlantic	UK	3,000 owners	4 resorts

Source: *Travel and Tourism Analyst* June 1986

Although timeshare in the UK has gone through a cautious period of investment in the mid-1980s these developments can bring spectacular rewards for the firms investing in them. For example the Palm Beach Club in Tenerife has 7,000 timeshare owners who have invested £43 million in 311 units. (TTA 1986).

The main timeshare developments have tended to be in those locations of the world where large volume tourism flows are already established, where there is a good year-round climate (so avoiding the problem of selling weeks during unseasonal periods), and where there are good links with the main tourism-generating countries. One good example is Fairfield Communities of the USA which is the world's largest timeshare developer. They have had timeshare sales of over $120 million in 5 years at Vistana, Florida, which is close to Disneyland in Orlando.

In Europe future timeshare developments are likely to focus on Greece, Spain and Portugal which are the least represented timeshare destinations. The main markets for timeshare sales will be West Germany (which is at present very underdeveloped) the UK and Scandinavia. All three countries are among the main users of the Mediterranean tourist destinations.

In the United States new timeshare developments have declined in number since the boom years of the early 1980s, although the more recent developments have been at a much larger scale, and several major corporations are investing in timeshare, including Marriott, Sheraton and ITT. The Major concentrations of timeshare resorts in the USA are in Florida, the Carolinas, and the California coast.

(vi) Leisure and Speciality Shopping in Indoor Resort Complexes

The future will see the development of large-scale mixed retail and leisure developments with tourism as the unique selling point. In northern latitudes all-weather complexes of this type will become the indoor resorts of the future. Shopping is an important adjunct to tourism. In 1986 tourist expenditure by overseas visitors to the UK on shopping accounted for 37 per cent of their total expenditure, emphasising the synergy of tourism investment with mixed development schemes.

West Edmonton Mall in Edmonton, Alberta, Canada provides a model for indoor resorts of the future. In 1981 it was originally intended to be a standard shopping centre but the owners decided to develop a theme park, an amusement park and shopping complex — all under one roof. It contains 836 shops, covers over 5 million square feet and cost over $600 million (U.S.) to build. At the centre is a 2½ acre lake with a replica Spanish galleon and 4 submarines (more than the Canadian Navy) that take visitors on an underwater ride through waters with live sharks and octopuses. The roof is 16 stories up. A 10 acre water park is now being built with a Fantasyland hotel. The whole complex employs 15,000 people and in 1985 brought in over $500 million (U.S.) revenue a year. There is parking for 30,000 cars. It now acts as a major visitor attraction in its own right and on autumn weekends over 400,000 visitors come to the Mall, nearly half of them from outside of Alberta. Many come from the United States on short break holidays. A third of visitors are now specifically attracted to Edmonton from the United States and the rest of Canada because of the West Edmonton Mall. In 1988 it attracted over 8 million visitors.

In London Battersea Power Station is being transformed into a family entertainment centre with high tech and heritage attractions on 8 floors. Being in the heart of London it goes beyond the traditional leisure park concept by providing a year round air conditioned weather proof environment, containing entertainments, restaurants and retail shops in one enormous complex. Over half the available space will be given over to rides, shows, attractions and arcades. Food and retailing will occupy about one-third of the space. It will cater for about 4.5 million visitors a year and will employ 4,000 people.

Europe's largest indoor shopping complex is the Metro Centre on Tyneside with 10,000 free car parking spaces and its own rail link to the centre of Newcastle. This huge shopping and entertainments complex is another indication of the type of development that can transform urban areas and lead to the emergence of the most unlikely tourist destinations.

For cities in northern latitudes with limited sunshine, large population concentrations and cheap land this may be the new type of tourist destination. Accessibility to large urban populations and new kinds of tourism product in an all-weather themed indoor environment will be the unique selling proposition that will enable those cities who invest to compete with the more traditional resort destinations.

(vii)   New Technology

Tourism probably more than any other industry is investing in new technology especially related to information services, booking and reservation systems and electronic transfer of data from cash (direct debits) to timetables. The cumbersome directories, timetables, and airline/shipping guides are rapidly being replaced by viewdata systems.

What is Viewdata? How does it work? Who uses it? Is there more than one system? These are some of the questions that might be asked and there is an array of answers to some of them. Viewdata is the electronic transmission of information on to a computer monitor screen via the telephone network. The scale of the technological revolution is impressive. Over 6,000 UK travel agents now have around 13,000 Viewdata terminals in use (TTG Jan 1987).

One major caveat to be made here is that the pace of technological development in travel and tourism in the UK has been so great over the past five years that any description risks becoming out of date as soon as it gets into print. One example is the speed with which the main UK tour operators have developed videotext information systems and computer networks. In 1982 all tour operators bookings were taken by telephone, telex or letter. By the end of 1986 Thomson, one of the big four tour operators, was able to insist that all agency bookings be made electronically. Some operators such as Horizon or Thomson have their own networks, but the three main UK videotext networks used in the travel industry are PRESTEL, ISTEL and FASTRAK. Airline reservation systems include TRAVICOM, SABRE and APOLLO.

The growth of videotext to become the major means of holiday reservations has also encouraged the growth of specialised databases covering a large number of subscribing tour operators. They are not confined to late booking but also used at peak booking periods. The three leading network suppliers ISTEL, FASTRAK and British Telecom Travel Service (which runs PRESTEL GATEWAY) have all invested big sums in preparation for the 1990 season. For example, two of the leading UK videotext operators ABC Electronic and ISTEL, have joined forces to give agents a new on-line service for package holidays and seat-only late availability. The new service called ABC Travelbank combines ISTEL's Travelbank and ABC's databases *Holidayfinder* and *Seatfinder* as well as offering instant cross connections to up to 30 tour operators connected to ISTEL. In addition, from April 1988 ABC Travelbank also carried ABC's International Travellers Guide, electronic mail, mailbox and telex facilities brochure requests, flight reservation systems and closed user group facilities.

Within the High Street travel agents over 95 per cent now use British Telecom's PRESTEL service which includes several pages of information supplied by the National Tourist Board (ETB). To enable small operators to access this material there is a low cost package available. In 1987 the English Tourist Board received more than a million accesses to their PRESTEL pages and processed over 50,000 orders for brochure packs for operators. PRESTEL is used by travel agents as a quick efficient way of getting news updates and for brochure ordering. For example, 85 per cent of 'top up' supplies of the England Holidays '88 brochure are now ordered via PRESTEL. The latest products on the PRESTEL service include British rail schedules and fares; information supplied by national and local tourist boards; hotel and UK resort information and live reservations; telex and electronic mail services; and a new theatre and concert reservation system.

In the case of the airlines, in order to fend off market penetration by the US systems the Association of European Airlines called for Europe's carriers to create a single European Computers Reservation System, but differences between two main factions has led to the development of two European-based international networks connecting their computers and the terminals of travel agents. Galileo is being developed by a consortia of airlines including British Airways, KLM, Swissair and Alitalia. Amadeus is the other consortium, set up by Air France, Lufthausa, SAS and Iberia. The aim of each consortium is to provide a complete information and transaction service to travel agents worldwide, to allow for up to the minute information, the issue of full documentation, recording and reporting of sales.

The most likely result is that in the UK, for example, that Galileo having British Airways as a major partner, is likely to become the major distribution network for travel agents, with a similar picture in Holland, Switzerland and Italy. Other systems will compete for the rest of the European market.

In the past 10 years Computer Reservation Systems in the United States have grown to such a scale that 88% of US airline tickets are sold through them. The growth of US air travel in the 1960s and 70s and its de-regulation in 1978 encouraged these processes. Airlines discovered that computer technology could help them keep up-to-date reservations and fares more accurately, quickly and cheaply than by taking on more clerical staff. The airlines quickly realised that an industry-wide reservations and fare system could be extended to retail travel agents especially the larger multiples developing the business travel market.

During the 1960s and 1970s there were several attempts to set up a single industry system but these largely failed because the two largest airlines — United and American said they would expand their own internal reservation systems and related products— Apollo and Sabre — and market them to travel agents. From

162

1976 the race was on to install CRS terminals at travel agent locations thus getting greater sales exposure. However the impact was relatively limited in a largely regulated market and the three largest airlines United, American and TWA also handled other carriers transactions.

However, after de-regulation in 1978, these joint activities ceased, particularly when the airlines began to realise the competitive edge they had in the form of their computerised reservation systems. A huge database is needed in order to process de-regulated fares and routes and the major carriers exploited their CRS's. For example fees per booking for smaller airlines were raised from 35 cents to $2.75 per booking.

A wide range of incentives were offered to agencies to sign up with the main systems — hardware, software, free lines and so on. The percentage of agencies with CRS went from 5% in 1977 to 95% as of May 1987. In theory use of automated airline systems didn't mean that agents had to lose their neutrality, but in practice they often did, as the airlines through financial penalties or pressure wrote contracts that precluded multiple systems.

In the 1980s this has resulted in growing interdependence between travel agents and airlines, high fees for previously very cheap services and agent favouritism. Other non-vendor airlines and agents began to complain on three major issues — fees, display bias and subscriber contracts. Fees were higher for CRS participants who competed with the vendor airlines and lower with CRS participants who didn't compete. Even where fees were paid there were charges of display bias in that the less competitive airlines were allegedly given better display positions. There was also the 'halo effect' that is higher revenues for airlines from their agents than from non-vendor agents which led to some substantial incentives being offered to agents. (In a 1985 Congressional hearing North Western cited an example of the incentives offered to an agent in its territory: $500,000 in cash, a 10% override (on top of the standard commission) for sales on United and five years free use of Apollo including telephone line charges if the agent would switch from Sabre to Apollo). In 1986 NorthWest resolved this by buying a half share in TWA's PARS system.

However, there are a number of lawsuits pending against United and American and to date the US Government has not acted. Sabre and Apollo between them now account for three quarters of automated revenue from airline ticket sales and CRS is clearly the primary form of marketing airline seats. (Table 29).

The 'halo effect' of CRS sales is certainly significant and the stronger airlines have found that the system dominating sales has the ability to affect sales. For ex-

Table 29:

Airline Computer Reservation Systems in the United States

Airline	American	United	Texas	TWA	Delta
CRS	Sabre	Apollo	System 1	Pars	Datas II
Revenue ($ millions)	490	325	210	160	140
Profits ($ millions)	190	125	50	40	20

ample American's Chairman, Robert Crandall, has said that American gained 8 – 12% in incremental revenue from display preference from Sabre Agents over non-Sabre automated agents.

Vast sums of money are involved in setting up CRS and they are now a major feature of airline strategic planning. American and United have spent about $750 million on Sabre and Apollo development and United has talked about $1 billion worth of new investment in computer systems and personnel. Texas Air is spending $200 to 400 million to make the System 1 CRS more competitive. In fact System 1 has been selected by the AMADEUS Consortium in Europe as the basis for their CRS. Each of the other main CRS's is investing heavily in order to increase or at least maintain their market share.

The impact of both de-regulation and CRS's on travel agents in the US has been considerable. The major CRS are looking for retail outlets who can bring them a large amount of business in the fastest possible time and that often means agents producing a lot of business travel. However, although there are over 29,000 travel agents in the US, only 7% of these accounted for 28% of agency sales and the picture has been one of fewer agents doing more business. In many cases dwindling profits have led to consolidation, and many agents have joined or formed chains that are able to offer good national coverage and the kinds of discounts on air tickets, hotel rooms and car rentals that came with volume of business. All CRS vendors are now offering agents PC's and three offer IBM's new PS/2 standard. These smart terminals offer a variety of accounting and administrative backup as well as the reservations system.

CONCLUSIONS

Advances in technology offer challenging and intriguing prospects in the years to come. The automation of office systems and indeed the development of electronic cash transfer, viewdata information and booking systems may in time lead to the disappearance of the high street retail travel agent. Brochures can be mailed direct to the home, where a teletext/viewdata system will enable the consumer to get instant information on holiday destinations and availability of bookings. He or she can then make their reservation and confirm by electronic direct-debit — all from the comfort of their own home. This will bring a new meaning to the phrase 'armchair traveller'.

Improvements in aircraft design and engineering projects such as the Channel Tunnel can transform holiday patterns. A new generation of wide-bodied jets which brings down the cost of long-haul travel will open up new markets for world tourism. China, for long inaccessible, is now being opened up to foreign tourists. (Over 1.7 million visited China in 1988), (China National Tourist Office 1989). As people's income and available leisure time increases, the tendency has been to take more short-break holidays, and the success of unlikely tourist destinations is evidence that the consumer is always seeking variety and cost-effective packages when considering holiday breaks.

The experiences gained by foreign travel encourage many tourists to repeat or extend their visits abroad. The domestic tourist industry must continue to be innovative in the force of foreign competition and in this industry more than any other, complacency will lead to a decline in business and ultimately firms going out of business. New products, new markets, harnessing the technology to improve operating costs and increase profit margins must all be sought after. The prospects are bright for the tourist industry in the 21st century. Many parts of the world have yet to realise their tourism potential and many new markets/new products are awaiting discovery.

ASSIGNMENTS

1. Identify what you think are the two most significant innovations in tourism during the 1980s. Give a measured justification for your choice.

2. Using your library, look at a tourist guide for the 1950s and compare it with one written in the 1980s. What are the main differences? What are the most significant changes that have taken place over the past 30 years?

References

CHAPTER 1

British Tourist Authority, (1984). *Annual Report.*
British Tourist Authority, (1986). *Annual Report.*
British Tourist Authority. *British National Travel Survey.* Annually.
British Tourist Authority *et al.* (1981) *Tourism in the UK — The Broad Perspective.*
Chicago Tribune, Graph, April 18, 1988.
Clawson, Marion and Carlton S. Van Doren. *Statistics on Outdoor Recreation.* Resources for the Future. Washington, D.C. 1984.
Department of Employment. *Pleasure, Leisure and Jobs — The Business of Tourism,* HMSO 1985.
Development of Tourism Act (1969) HMSO 1969.
English Tourist Board, (1986). *Annual Report.*
English Tourist Board. *Annual Reports and Regional Facts Sheets.*
Frechtling, Douglas. 'U.S. Domestic Holiday Traffic,' Travel and Tourism Analyst. *The Economist* Publications. London. 1986.
The Henley Centre. *Leisure Futures,* Published quarterly.
International Union of Official Travel Organisations (IUOTO). *UN Conference on International Travel and Tourism,* Rome 1963.
International Passenger Survey. (Published annually, usually reported in *British Business).*
League of Nations. *Report on Tourism by Committee of Statistical Experts,* January 1937.
Lickorish, L.J. *The Travel Trade.* 1958, Appendix III.
National Tourism Resources Review Commission, Report: *Destination USA.* Six Volumes. Washington, D.C. 1973.
Organisation for Economic Cooperation and Development. *Tourism Policy and International Tourism.* Published annually. ECD Paris.
Time Magazine: 'Travel--A $260 Billion U.S. Industry on the Move,' Magazine, Business Edition, May 18, 1987.
Travel Weekly. *Travel Market Yearbook, 1987.* News Group Publishing. 1986.
U.S. Department of Commerce. International Travel and Passenger Fares, 1982, *Survey of Current Business* 63, No. 5, May 1983.
U.S. Department of Commerce. International Travel and Passenger Fares, 1986, *Survey of Current Business,* 67, No. 6, June 1987.
U.S.A. Snapshots, *U.S.A. Today* December 5, 1984.
U.S.A. Snapshots, *U.S.A. Today* May 5, 1986.
U.S. Travel Data Center. *National Travel Survey*--Full Year Report 1986. Washington, D.C. 1987.
U.S. Travel Data Center. *The 1986–87 Economic Review of Travel in America.* Washington, D.C. 1987.
U.S. Travel and Tourism Administration. *Recap of International Travel to and from the United States in 1986.* U.S. Department of Commerce, Washington, D.C. 1987.
Waters, S.R. *Travel Industry World Yearbook*--The Big Picture. (1987). Child and Waters. New York. 1987.
Waters, S.R. *Travel Industry World Yearbook*--The Big Picture. (1988) Child and Waters. New York. 1987.
White, K. and M. Walker. 'Trouble in the Travel Account' *Annals of Tourism Research 1982.*

World Tourism Organisation. *Annual Reports.*
World Tourism Organisation. *Economic Review of World Tourism,* WTO 1986.
World Tourism Organisation. *World Tourism Statistics Annual Yearbook.*

CHAPTER 2

Bennett, E.D. (Ed.) *American Journeys-An Anthology of Travel in the United States.* Convent Station, New Jersey: Travel Vision. 1975.

British Travel Association. *The British Travel Association 1929 – 1969,* British Tourist Authority 1970.

Brittain J. and E. Wedlake Brayley. *The Beauties of England and Wales,* (Cumberland) London 1802.

Brunner, E. *Holiday Making and the Holiday Trades,* OUP 1945.

Burnet, L. *Villegiature et Tourisme sur les Cotes de France,* Paris 1963.

Clawson, Marion. The Crisis in Outdoor Recreation. American Forests 65(3):22 – 31, (1959).

Defort, P.P. 'Quelques Reperes Historique du Tourisme Moderne'. *The Tourism Review,* January/March 1958.

De Santis, Hugh. The Democratization of Travel: The Travel Agent in American History. *Journal of American Culture* 1(1):1 – 17, (1978).

Dulles, Foster Rhea. A History of Recreation-America Learns to Play. New York: Appleton-Century-Crofts. 1965.

Howell, Sara. *The Seaside.* Cassell, Collier, MacMillan, London. 1974.

Lennard, R. *Englishmen at Rest and Play,* Clarendon Press. Oxford, 1931.

Lickorish, L.J. and A.G. Kershaw. *op. cit.* Chap. 1.

Lundberg, Donald E. *The Hotel and Restaurant Business.* CBI-Van Nostrand, New York. 1984.

Lundberg, Donald E. *The Tourist Business.* Cahner Books, Boston. 1974, 1985.

Patmore, J.A. *Land and Leisure,* David and Charles 1970.

Smollett, T. *Humphrey Clinker,* Dent.

Stephenson, R.L. *Travels with a donkey in the Cevennes,* Dent 1986.

Swinglehurst, Edmund. *Cook's Tours-The Story of Popular Travel.* Blandford Press. Poole, Dorset. 1982.

Travel Weekly. Travel Weekly's 25th Anniversary Issue. (May 31) 1983.

Travel Weekly. Park Data Show RV's Top Choice. (September 3) 1984.

Ullman, Edward L. 1954, Amenities as a Factor in Regional Growth. The Geographical Review 44(2):119 – 132.

U.S. Bureau of the Census, *Statistical Abstract of the United States.* Washington, D.C. Various years.

Van Doren, Carlton S. 1981, Outdoor Recreation Trends in the 1980s: Implications for Society. *Journal of Travel Research* 19:3 – 10.

Van Doren, Carlton S. 1983, The Future of Tourism. *Journal of Physical Education, Recreation and Dance* 54:27 – 29. 42.

Van Doren, Carlton S. 'The Consequences of Forty Years of Tourism Growth,' *Annals of Tourism Research,* 12, 1985.

CHAPTER 3

Cohen, Erik. 'Rethinking the Sociology of Tourism,' *Annals of Tourism Research.* 6 No. 1, Jan/March 1979.

Caribbean Tourism Research and Development Center, 1987. *Travel and Leisure's World Tourism Overview 1987/1988,* The Annual Review of the Travel Industry World Wide, American Express Publishing Company, NY. 1987.

Education and Training Advisory Council. *Hotel and Catering Skills — Now and in the Future,* Hotel and Catering Industry Training Board, London 1983.

Gearing, Charles E. *et al. Planning for Tourism Development,* Praeger Publishers. 1976.

Gunn, Clare A. *Vacationscape-Designing Tourist Regions,* Second Edition. Van Nostrand. 1988.

Gunn, Clare A. *Tourism Planning,* Second Edition. Taylor and Francis. 1988.

Institute of Manpower Studies. *Jobs in Tourism and Leisure,* English Tourist Board 1986.

Mayo, Edward J. and Lance P. Jarvis. *The Psychology of Leisure Travel.* CBI Publishing. 1981.

McIntosh, Robert W. and Charles R. Goeldner. *Tourism--Principles, Practices, Philosophies.* Wiley & Sons, New York. 1986.

Plog, Stanley. 'Why Destination Areas Rise and Fall in Popularity,' *Cornell HRA Quarterly* 14 No. 4. 1974.

Ritchie, J.R. Brent and Charles R. Goeldner. *Travel, Tourism and Hospitality Research.* New York: John Wiley and Sons. 1987.

Stengel, Richard. 'Ah, Wilderness!' America's parks have become too popular for their own good,' *Time,* July 11, 1988.

Time Magazine, 'Travel--A $260 Billion U.S. Industry on the Move,' Business Edition, May 18, 1987.

Travel Weekly. *Travel Market Yearbook, 1987.* News Group Publishing. 1986.

Travel Weekly. *Waikiki Beach and Oahu--1988 Reference Guide* (Supplement). July 11, 1988.

U.S. Department of Interior. *National Park Statistical Abstract.* 1987. Denver, Colorado.

U.S. Travel Data Center. *Tourism's Top Twenty* (1987). Washington, D.C. 1987.

Waters, S.R. *Travel Industry World Yearbook*--The Big Picture. (1987). Child and Waters. New York. 1987.

Waters, S.R. *Travel Industry World Yearbook*--The Big Picture. (1988) Child and Waters. New York. 1987.

CHAPTER 4

Working group of the National Trust Organisations of the EEC, Fifth Report *The Economic Significance of Tourism within the European Economic Community. British Tourist Authority, 1983.*

Organisation for Economic Cooperation and Development. op. cit.

Waters, S.R. (Ed). *op. cit.* Chap. 1.

World Tourism Organisation. *Economic Review of World Tourism,* WTO 1986.

CHAPTER 5

American Society of Travel Agents. *ASTA. STAT.* Various issues.

Beaver, A. *Mind Your Own Travel Business,* Beaver Travel 1979.

Business Travel News, 1988 Business Travel Survey, Issue 113, CMP Publications, June 6, 1988, I.

Economist Intelligence Unit. *The British Travel Industry — A Survey, London 1968.*

Lickorish, L.J. and A.G. Kershaw. The Travel Trade. 1958.

The Times, Article in the Business section 12.1.87.

Travel Trade Gazette, Article, January 1987.

'The 1988 Louis Harris Survey.' *Travel Weekly,* June 29, 1988.

Travel Weekly Focus, '1987 Profit Guide,' July 31, 1987.

CHAPTER 6

Beeching Report. *The Reshaping of British Railways.*

Department of Trade. *Report of Official Inquiry into the collapse of the Court Line,* HMSO 1975.

Daube, Scott. 'Daylight Rockies Service Debust,' *Travel Weekly,* July 21, 1988, 24.

Lickorish, L.J. *op. cit.* Chap. 1.

Official Airline Guides (OAG). *Worldwise Cruise and Shipline Guide* (bi-monthly).

The Travel Agent, 'More Americans Take to the Skies,' October 19, 1987.

Time Magazine, 'Travel--A $260 Billion U.S. Industry on the Move,' Business Edition, May 18, 1987.

Transport Act 1980.

Transport Act 1988.

Transport Statistics, HMS (Annually).

Travel Agent Magazine, 'ABA's Top 100 List Rounds Up Cream of North America's Crop,' March 3, 1988.

United States Travel Data Centre — Annual Surveys of Airline Travellers to US.

Waters, S.R. *Travel Industry World Yearbook*--The Big Picture. (1987). Child and Waters. New York. 1987.

Waters, S.R. *Travel Industry World Yearbook*--The Big Picture. (1988) Child and Waters. New York. 1987.

CHAPTER 7

Brown, B. and P. Lavery. *A survey of serviced and self-catering accommodation in South East Dorset,* Southern Tourist Board 1986.

Department of Employment. *Action for Jobs* in Tourism HMSO 1986.

Education and Training Advisory Council. *Hotel and Catering Skills — Now and in the Future,* Hotel and Catering Training Board 1983.

FOA/ECE Working Party on Agrarian Structure and Farm Rationalisation (Several papers on Farm Tourism contained in) *Report of the Symposium on Agriculture and Tourism,* Government of Finland, Helsinki 1982.

Horwath and Horwath. *World Wide Hotel Industry.* 1987.

Laventhol and Horwath. *U.S. Lodging Industry* 1986. Philadelphia. 1986.

Travel Weekly, 'Study Cities Need for More Hotel Rooms.' November 11, 1985. 44 No. 103, 1985.

U.S. Department of Interior. *National Park Statistical Abstract,* 1987. Denver, Colorado.

U.S. Travel Data Center. *National Travel Survey*--Full Year Report 1986. Washington, D.C. 1987.

Waters, S.R. *Travel Industry World Yearbook*--The Big Picture. (1987). Child and Waters. New York. 1987.

CHAPTER 8

British Tourist Authority, 1970.

Beekhuis, Jeanne V. *World Travel Overview.* Travel and Leisure 1987 – 1988.

Department of Employment. *Pleasure, Leisure and Jobs* (Ch 4) *op. cit.*

English Tourist Board. *Annual Reports.*

Hewett, R, and L.J. Lickorish et al. The British Travel Association 1929 – 1969, London 1971.

National Tourism Resources Review Commission, Report: *Destination USA.* Six Volumes. Washington, D.C. 1973.

Organization for Economic Cooperation and Development, *Tourism Policy and Inter national Tourism.* Paris. 1984.

United States Congress. National Tourism Policy Act. 97th Congress 1st Session (Public Law 97–63). 1981.

U.S. Travel Data Center. *The 1986–87 Economic Review of Travel in America. Washington, D.C. 1987.*

CHAPTER 9

British Tourist Authority. *Strategy for Growth 1984–88,* 1984.

English Tourist Board, *Financing Tourist Projects,* 1980.

Further developments on the Languedoc Rousillion development, see:

Lavery, P. *et al. The Strategy for Hadrians Wall,* Countryside Commission 1984.

Loudry, R. 'Tourism development of Languedoc Rousillon'. Paper given at International Seminar *Physical Planning and Area Development for Tourism,* IUOTO Geneva 1973.

Lundberg, Donald E. *The Tourist Business.* Cahner Books, Boston. 1974, 1985.

Murphy, Peter. *Tourism A Community Approach.* Methuen. 1985.

Tourism U.S.A. Guidelines for Tourism Development. U.S. Department of Commerce, U.S. Travel and Tourism Administration. 1986.

Travel Weekly. Waikiki Beach and Oahu--1988 Reference Guide (Supplement). July 11, 1988.

CHAPTER 10

For further reading on Tourism Marketing, see:

Foster, D. *Travel and Tourism Management,* Macmillan 1985.

Krippendorf. *Marketing et Tourisme,* H. Lang & Co 1971.

Wahab, S. *et al. Tourism Marketing,* Tourism International Press 1976.

CHAPTER 11

Archer, B. & C.B. Owen. Towards a Tourist Regional Multiplier 1971.

Isard, W. *Methods of Regional Analysis,* MIT (1969).

Organisation for Economic Cooperation and Development. *Tourism Policy and Inter national Tourism.* Published annually.

Richardson, H. *Elements of Regional Economics,* Penguin (1970).

U.S. Department of Commerce. International Travel and Passenger Fares, 1982. *Survey of Current Business* 63, No. 5, May 1983.

U.S. Department of Commerce. International Travel and Passenger Fares, 1986, *Survey of Current Business,* 67, No. 6, June 1987.

CHAPTER 12

Burton, R. *Recreation Carrying Capacity in the Countryside,* MSc Thesis, University of Birmingham, 1974.

Ceton, Marvin J., *et al.* 'Into the 21st Century, Long Term Trends Affecting the United States.' *The Futurist,* Vol. 22:4 July-August, 1988.

Davis, Robert S. 'Tuttle Cites the Importance of Regional Structure,' *Travel Weekly,* Vol. 45:96, November 3, 1986.

De Santis, Hugh. The Democratization of Travel: The Travel Agent in American History, *Journal of American Culture,* 1(1):1 – 17, 1978.

Dower, M. and P.E. McCarthy. 'Planning for Conservation and Development', *Journal of the Royal Town Planning Institute,* 53, No. 1, 1967.

European Information Centre for Nature Conservation *The Management of the En vironment in Tomorrow's Europe,* Council of Europe, Strasbourg, 1971.

Furmidge, J. 'Planning for Recreation in the Countryside'. *Journal of the Royal Town Planning Institute,* 55, No. 2, 1969.

Houghton-Evans, W. and J.C. Miles 'Environmental Capacity in Rural Recreation Areas', *Journal of the Royal Town Planning Institute,* 56, No. 10, 1970.

Kotler, Philip. Dream Vacation—The Booming Market for Designing Experiences. The Futurist 18:5, 1984.

Organisation for Economic Cooperation and Development. *The Impact of Tourism on the Environment,* General Report OECD, Paris 1980.

Ragatz, Richard L. Trends in the Market for Privately Owned Seasonal Recreational Housing. Proceedings — 1980 National Outdoor Recreation Trends Symposium, Volume 2, U.S. Department of Agriculture, Forest Service, Northeastern Forest Ex periment Station, Broomall, PA, General Technical Report N.E.—57, 1980.

Van Doren, Carton S. Outdoor Recreation Trends in the 1980s : implications for Society. Journal of Travel Research 19:3 – 10, 1981.

Van Doren, Carlton S. 'The Consequences of Forty Years of Tourism Growth,' *Annals of Tourism Research,* 12, 1985.

173

PRACTICAL EXERCISES FOR GROUPS SERIES (PEG)

Series editor: Humphrey Shaw
Consultant Programmers: Jon Carter   Brian Dakin   Wayne Griffiths

The PEG Series has been designed for trainee managers and students of
& management studies to assist them in developing their analytical
& problem solving skills. The Series comprises two main parts.

- 1 -

PEG Master Series

issn 0954-030X

Case studies & Tutor's Manuals

There are 2 books of case studies, which introduce financial & quantitative
management and to entrepreneurial decision making. Suitable for
both individual and group working, they cover a range of business problems
and are ideal for student-centred learning.

Decision making : case studies in financial & quantitative management
30 varied & topical small case studies. Book £4.95 isbn 0 946139 42 3
Tutor's Manual (model answers etc) £49.99 (free with 15 books direct)
isbn 0 946139 47 4
Entrepreneurial decision making has 50 case studies on enterprise & business
for BTEC & other post-experience courses. Book £4.95 isbn 0 946139 69 5
Tutor's Manual (model answers etc) £49.99 (free with 15 books direct)
isbn 0 946139 74 1

Computer simulations

The Football Manager Simulation offers hands-on computer experience,
working on a a range of financial, personnel and marketing problems.
The House Building Simulation encourages group working in running a
property building company and making all the important decisions.
It is ideally suitable for residential courses, and for in-class work.

The Restaurant Manager Simulation will be ready at Easter, 1990.

Simulations (on 5¼" or 3½" disk compatible with most IBM & lookalike PCs)
are £99.99+VAT including Tutor's Manual; Educational versions
are £49.99+VAT including Tutor's Manual

STARTING WORK SERIES (issn 0953-0959)

Series editors: Sheila McCallum and Anne Strong

The Starting Work series offers modern, practical coverage of the basic tasks done by young people in a variety of workplaces. Both books are aimed at 16-18 year olds who are on pre-vocational or vocational courses in further education or at a private training school.

Starting Work in Sales

No. 1 in the Series   £7.95   isbn 0 946139 22 9

The student is shown how to acquire a wide range of retail skills by exercises based on the departments of a large store. Topics covered include product knowledge, customer service, health and safety, finance, design and layout, marketing and consumer law.

Tutor's Manual of notes, model answers, colour slides, overhead transparencies etc to support the textbook. isbn 0 946139 27 X

Starting Work in the Salon

No. 2 in the Series   £7.95   isbn 0 946139 32 6

Students are shown how to get a job in a hairdressing salon, and are taken through such tasks and exercises as doing the salon laundry, hygiene, customer contact, reception duties, cutting, perming, availability of hair products, salon design and layout and contracts of employment. Photographs from working salons add depth to the text and give further insights into the day to day running of a salon.

T utor's Manual of notes, illustrations, exercises, overhead projection transparencies and other materials to support the text. isbn 0 946139 37 7

CASE STUDIES IN MANAGEMENT

private sector, introductory level

second edition

edited by Sheila Ritchie

A topical and interesting collection of real-life business
case studies based on mainly small and medium-sized
companies. There are nine mini-cases (short incident
studies) and ten longer, cross-functional cases.
There is an interesting mix of products and services, from
chemicals and valves to books and leisure.

Sewn paperback   £7.95   isbn 0 946139 02 4

TUTOR'S PACK

The Tutor's Pack comprises model answers, notes and
other materials (including some computer programs and 6
overhead projector transparencies). All cases in the book
have been tested on business management students and
the notes in the Tutor's Pack build on that experience.

Bound in a presentation file with loose insert plastic pockets
£49.00 (gratis with 15 copies of the book bought direct)

isbn 0 946139 07 5

MRS THATCHER'S CASEBOOK

Non-partisan studies in Conservative Government policy

Terry Garrison

Well-researched case studies of ten major crises handled
by Mrs Thatcher's government.

Inner city time bomb ?
The Falklands War
GCHQ
Deregulation of the buses
London Transport - Fares Fair
The coal strike
Flexible rostering - British Rail
British Steel
The De Lorean dream
British Leyland

Includes a large section on policy analysis for managers.

Hardback binding   £12.95   isbn 0 946139 86 5

TUTOR'S PACK

Case notes, chronologies, commentary and other material
to supplement, support and extend the text.

A4 binder: copying rights £39.00 (free with 15+ books direct)
isbn 0 946139 46 6

A Manager's Guide to Quantitative Methods

Michael Cuming

isbn 0 946139 01 6   £8.90   Paperback

An unusual and comprehensive introduction to
quantitative methods using topical examples
and diagrams to analyse real problems
and suggest solutions.

A user-friendly book for managers who need
to appreciate the uses, misuses and potentialities
of quantitative methods.

CONTENTS

'Overall this book is a comprehensive guide to quantitative
methods and *truly should require no previous mathematical
knowledge...* It is worth serious consideration for
a wide range of management courses.
V.J. Seddon in *Natfhe Journal* February, 1985.

People in organisations

Pat Armstrong & Chris Dawson

BOOK

A standard introductory text to the management of people at work, specially written for the BTEC business studies course at HNC/D level and used by many colleges on their DMS stage 1, IPM, IWM CMS and other first level supervisory and management courses. Used by numerous colleges as a set textbook and by the Institute of Bankers for their diploma course recommended reading list.

CONTENTS

Organisational goals: determinants of/variations in structure
Human resource planning
Personality/attitude formation & change
The motivation to work/communication & perception
Groups/leadership
Acquiring new employees/recruitment & selection
Psychological testing/the interview
Human resource planning and control techniques
Learning/training
Rewards
Industrial relations/legislation on IR
The organisation in context/systems/technology/change

isbn 0 946139 55 5   £6.90   Sewn paperback   Published January, 1989

TUTOR'S PACK

10 classroom-tested exercises based on a simulated company with model answers, notes and other materials to support and extend the book. Carries copying rights of student materials for purchasers.

isbn 0 946139 60 1   £19.00 (free with 15+ books bought direct) Jan., 1989